OSLO TR
GUID

2023 and beyond

A Comprehensive Guide To Norway's Captivating Capital: Explore Oslo's Rich History, Iconic Landmarks, Cultural Treasures And Natural Wonders.

By

Williams Carter

TABLE OF CONTENT

CHAPTER FOUR

CHAPTER FIVE

CHAPTER SIX

CHATER SEVEN

CHAPTER EIGHT

CHAPTER NINE

CHAPTER TEN

CHAPTER ELEVEN

PRACTICAL INFORMATION AND TIPS

CHAPTER TWELVE

CONCLUSION

CHAPTER ONE

Introduction to Oslo

1.1 Welcome to Oslo:

Welcome to the vibrant city of Oslo, the capital of Norway and a true gem of Scandinavia. Nestled between the Oslofjord and lush green hills, Oslo beckons with its picturesque setting and captivating allure. As you step foot in this enchanting city, you'll immediately be embraced by a sense of wonder and anticipation, as Oslo unfolds its treasures before your eyes.

The natural beauty of Oslo is simply awe-inspiring. The Oslofjord, with its sparkling blue waters, stretches out invitingly, providing a stunning backdrop for the city. The fjord offers a myriad of opportunities for exploration, from leisurely boat trips to thrilling water sports. As you venture along the shoreline, you'll discover idyllic beaches, charming islands, and quaint fishing villages, each imbued with its own distinct character and story.

But Oslo's allure extends far beyond its fjord. Lush green hills and verdant forests envelop the city, creating a serene and tranquil atmosphere. As you wander through these natural havens, you'll encounter meandering trails, hidden lakes, and panoramic viewpoints that offer breathtaking vistas of the cityscape. Whether you're an avid hiker, a nature enthusiast, or simply seeking solace in the embrace of the outdoors, Oslo's abundant green spaces will captivate your heart.

The architectural wonders of Oslo are another testament to the city's allure. A harmonious blend of old and new, Oslo's skyline boasts an eclectic mix of architectural styles. From the medieval fortress of Akershus to the grandeur of the Royal Palace, from the contemporary elegance of the Oslo Opera House to the iconic slopes of the Holmenkollen Ski Jump, Oslo's buildings tell a story of the city's past and present.

Culture aficionados will find themselves immersed in a treasure trove of artistic and historical wonders. Oslo is home to world-class museums, galleries, and cultural institutions that showcase the nation's rich heritage. The National Gallery proudly displays Edvard Munch's iconic painting, "The Scream," while the Munch Museum offers a deeper exploration into the life and works of this renowned Norwegian artist. The Oslo Cathedral, with its graceful architecture and serene ambiance, invites contemplation and reflection, while the Nobel Peace Center pays homage to the ideals of peace and humanitarianism.

Beyond the tangible attractions, Oslo's warm hospitality and welcoming atmosphere will make you feel right at home. The locals, known for their friendly nature and genuine kindness, will gladly share their love for their city, providing insider tips and recommendations that will enhance your experience. Oslo's vibrant cultural scene, buzzing with music festivals, art exhibitions, and theatrical performances, ensures that there's always something exciting happening around every corner.

Prepare to be enchanted by Oslo, where natural beauty, rich history, and modern charm converge to create a truly unforgettable experience. Let the captivating landscapes, architectural marvels, cultural treasures, and warm hospitality of Oslo leave an indelible mark on your journey, as you uncover the wonders that make this city a true gem of Scandinavia.

1.2 Oslo's Rich History:

Oslo's fascinating history spans over a millennium, beginning with its humble origins as a Viking settlement in the 11th century. Initially known as Ánslo, the city gradually grew in importance due to its strategic location along trade routes and its proximity to natural resources. As the years passed, Oslo transformed into a bustling trading hub, attracting merchants from far and wide during the Middle Ages.

In 1314, Oslo became the capital of Norway, solidifying its position as a center of power and governance. Over the centuries, the city witnessed the rise and fall of various kingdoms, including the reign of the Kalmar Union, which united Denmark, Norway, and Sweden under one monarch. This period marked significant developments in trade, culture, and governance, leaving lasting influences on Oslo's identity.

However, Oslo's journey was not without challenges. Throughout its history, the city faced devastating fires that ravaged its wooden structures, requiring extensive rebuilding efforts. The most notable fire occurred in 1624, when a substantial portion of the city was destroyed. This event led to the decision to relocate and rebuild the city under the name Christiania, named after King Christian IV. The name persisted until 1925, when the city reclaimed its original name, Oslo.

Oslo also endured the impacts of war and conflicts. During the Napoleonic Wars, Norway was under Danish rule, and the city became a crucial strategic location. It experienced occupation by Swedish and Danish forces, as well as conflicts with neighboring countries. In the 20th century, Oslo witnessed the German occupation during World War II, which left its mark on the city and its people.

Despite these challenges, Oslo's resilience shone through. Each setback fueled the city's determination to rebuild and preserve its cultural heritage. Today, visitors can witness remnants of the past scattered throughout the city. From the imposing Akershus Fortress, which played a significant role in defending Oslo throughout history, to the well-preserved historical districts of Gamlebyen and Kvadraturen, Oslo offers a rich tapestry of architectural treasures and cultural landmarks that reflect its evolving identity.

Exploring Oslo's historical sites provides a captivating journey through time. The Oslo Cathedral, with its Gothic architecture and centuries-old history, stands as a symbol of the city's religious heritage. The Royal Palace, home to the Norwegian royal family, offers a glimpse into the country's monarchical history and regal traditions. Meanwhile, the Viking Ship Museum houses remarkably preserved Viking ships, testaments to Norway's seafaring past and the ingenuity of its ancestors.

By delving into Oslo's history, visitors gain profound insights into the city's evolution, resilience, and the events that have shaped Norway's national identity. Whether strolling through the medieval alleyways of Bryggen, where the echoes of Hanseatic merchants still linger, or exploring the artifacts and exhibits in the numerous museums, Oslo's historical heritage is alive and waiting to be discovered.

1.3 Oslo Today: A Modern Scandinavian Metropolis:

While deeply rooted in its history, Oslo has also embraced the modern era with open arms, becoming a thriving metropolis that harmoniously blends tradition and innovation. With its forward-thinking mindset, Oslo has consistently ranked as one of the world's most livable cities, renowned for its sustainable urban planning, high quality of life, and progressive values.

As you wander through Oslo's streets, you'll notice striking architectural masterpieces coexisting alongside picturesque parks and waterfront promenades. The city's contemporary skyline is dominated by sleek glass structures, including the iconic Oslo Opera House and cutting-edge museums that reflect Norway's commitment to design and creativity.

Oslo's architectural prowess is evident in its commitment to both functionality and aesthetics. The Oslo Opera House, designed by Snøhetta, is a prime example of the city's architectural innovation. Its unique, angular structure resembles an iceberg floating on the Oslofjord, inviting visitors to explore its interior and providing a stunning backdrop for performances. The Oslo Barcode Project, a collection of modern high-rise buildings, showcases the city's dedication to sustainable design and energy efficiency. These architectural marvels not only enhance the city's skyline but also create vibrant spaces for culture, commerce, and leisure.

Beyond its architectural allure, Oslo is a hub of innovation and creativity. The city is home to a thriving startup scene, attracting entrepreneurs and investors from around the world. The combination of a supportive business environment, access to capital, and a highly educated workforce has fostered a culture of entrepreneurship and technological advancement. Startups in fields such as clean energy, biotechnology, and fintech are flourishing, contributing to Oslo's reputation as a global center for innovation.

In addition to its entrepreneurial spirit, Oslo boasts world-class research institutions and universities. These institutions drive groundbreaking research across various fields, including sustainability, marine sciences, and renewable energy. Oslo's commitment to research and development has resulted in numerous scientific breakthroughs and collaborations with international partners.

Oslo's dedication to sustainability goes hand in hand with its innovative mindset. The city has implemented ambitious plans to reduce carbon emissions and combat climate change. From an extensive public transportation network to an emphasis on cycling infrastructure, Oslo prioritizes eco-friendly modes of transportation. The city also promotes energy-efficient buildings, waste management systems, and renewable energy sources. By prioritizing sustainability, Oslo sets an example for other cities worldwide, demonstrating that economic growth and environmental stewardship can coexist.

As you delve deeper into Oslo's cultural scene, you'll discover a city that cherishes its artistic heritage while embracing contemporary expressions. The city is teeming with art galleries, showcasing works from both local and international artists. The Astrup Fearnley Museum of Modern Art and the Munch Museum are must-visit destinations for art enthusiasts, housing collections that span various artistic movements and mediums.

Theater and performing arts thrive in Oslo, with a rich calendar of performances throughout the year. The Oslo Opera House, in addition to its architectural significance, hosts world-class opera and ballet productions. The city's theaters offer a diverse range of performances, from classic plays to experimental theater. Oslo's music scene is equally vibrant, catering to all tastes and genres. From intimate jazz clubs to large concert arenas, you'll find a plethora of live music venues hosting both local talents and international acts.

Food lovers will relish Oslo's dynamic culinary landscape, which celebrates both traditional Norwegian cuisine and international flavors. Local ingredients take center stage, with fresh seafood sourced from the fjords, wild game from the forests, and seasonal produce from local farms. Whether you're indulging in a seafood feast at a waterfront restaurant, exploring the stalls of Mathallen Food Hall, or sampling Nordic-inspired fusion dishes, Oslo offers a gastronomic adventure that will delight your taste buds.

Oslo's commitment to nature and outdoor pursuits is woven into the fabric of the city. The proximity to forests, lakes, and the Oslofjord allows residents and visitors to easily escape into nature without venturing far from the city center. Outdoor activities abound, offering opportunities for hiking, biking, kayaking, and fishing. The Nordmarka forest, located just a short distance from downtown Oslo, is a popular destination for nature enthusiasts. Its network of trails offers breathtaking views, serene lakes, and a chance to reconnect with the tranquility of the wilderness.

Oslo's dedication to preserving its natural surroundings extends to its numerous parks and green spaces. From the expansive Vigeland Park, adorned with Gustav Vigeland's iconic sculptures, to the botanical gardens of Tøyen Park, Oslo's parks provide havens of serenity and beauty. These green oases offer opportunities for picnics, leisurely strolls, and outdoor concerts, inviting both locals and visitors to bask in the harmony of urban and natural landscapes.

In conclusion, Oslo's ability to embrace its rich history while embracing innovation and sustainability is a testament to its unique character. The city's architectural wonders, vibrant cultural scene, culinary delights, and commitment to nature make it a must-visit destination for travelers seeking a harmonious blend of tradition and modernity. Whether you're exploring its museums, savoring its culinary creations, or immersing yourself in its natural splendor, Oslo promises an unforgettable experience that showcases the very best of Scandinavian charm and progressive values.

As you delve into this comprehensive Oslo travel guide, prepare to uncover the captivating history, vibrant present, and boundless possibilities that await you in this modern Scandinavian metropolis. Oslo invites you to immerse yourself in its unique blend of culture, natural splendor, and cosmopolitan flair, promising an unforgettable journey of discovery.

CHAPTER TWO

Planning Your Trip to Oslo

2.1 Best Time to Visit Oslo

Oslo, the capital of Norway, offers a unique experience throughout the year, each season highlighting different aspects of the city. Here are the distinct seasons and their highlights to help you choose the best time to visit:

Spring (March to May):

Spring in Oslo is a delightful season marked by the awakening of nature after the long winter. As the temperatures start to rise, the cityscape is adorned with colorful flowers and budding trees, creating a vibrant atmosphere. The mild weather makes it a pleasant time to explore Oslo's outdoor spaces and indulge in various activities.

One of the must-visit places during spring in Oslo is Vigeland Park. Located within Frogner Park, this iconic sculpture park boasts over 200 captivating statues created by Gustav Vigeland. As you stroll through the park's pathways lined with blooming flowers, you'll be immersed in the artistic ambiance and the intricate beauty of the sculptures.

Spring is also an ideal time for outdoor enthusiasts to engage in cycling and hiking adventures. Oslo offers a range of picturesque trails and paths that wind through forests, along lakeshores, and up the city's hills. The Bygdøy Peninsula is a popular destination for nature lovers, offering serene coastal walks and lush green landscapes.

Additionally, the longer daylight hours in spring allow for extended exploration of Oslo's attractions. You can visit historic landmarks like Akershus Fortress, take a leisurely boat ride on the Oslo Fjord, or simply relax in one of the city's many parks and gardens.

Summer (June to August):

Summer is a vibrant and energetic season in Oslo, with long, sunny days and a bustling atmosphere. It is the peak tourist season, as visitors from around the world flock to the city to enjoy the pleasant weather and participate in numerous outdoor events and festivities.

During the summer months, Oslo transforms into a cultural hub, with a multitude of festivals, concerts, and cultural events taking place. The Oslo Jazz Festival, the Øyafestivalen music festival, and the Oslo Pride Parade are just a few examples of the vibrant celebrations that fill the city's streets and parks.

One of the highlights of summer in Oslo is the lively street markets. The most famous of these is the Mathallen Food Hall, where you can sample a variety of local delicacies, artisanal products, and international cuisine. The markets also showcase local arts and crafts, providing an excellent opportunity to browse and purchase unique souvenirs.

Exploring Oslo's outdoor attractions is a popular activity during the summer season. Take a boat tour on the Oslo Fjord to enjoy breathtaking views of the surrounding islands and coastal landscapes. The fjord offers opportunities for swimming, kayaking, and fishing, allowing you to make the most of the warm weather.

Additionally, summer in Oslo is synonymous with the vibrant café culture. The city is dotted with charming outdoor cafés where you can savor a cup of coffee or indulge in a delicious Norwegian pastry while immersing yourself in the lively street scenes and enjoying the pleasant temperatures.

Autumn (September to November):

Autumn in Oslo is a season of enchanting beauty as nature transforms into a kaleidoscope of vibrant colors. The mild weather and the decreasing crowds make it an excellent time to explore the city's cultural attractions, immerse yourself in local culture, and witness the stunning autumn scenery.

Oslo's parks and gardens, such as Ekebergparken and the Botanical Gardens, become a haven of autumnal splendor during this time of year. The trees don their fiery hues of red, orange, and gold, creating a picturesque backdrop for leisurely walks and picnics.

Museums and art galleries also come alive during autumn, offering a refuge for rainy days and a deeper understanding of Norwegian culture. The National Gallery, home to Edvard Munch's iconic painting "The Scream," is a must-visit for art enthusiasts. Other notable museums include the Munch Museum, the Viking Ship Museum, and the Nobel Peace Center.

As the temperatures begin to cool, autumn in Oslo is an opportunity to experience local traditions and festivities. Celebrate the harvest season by visiting farmers' markets, where you can sample fresh produce, traditional Norwegian dishes, and homemade preserves. You may also have the chance to witness traditional folk dances and music performances, showcasing the rich cultural heritage of Norway.

Winter (December to February):

Winter in Oslo is a magical time, with the city transformed into a winter wonderland. While the temperatures may be cold, the festive atmosphere and the array of winter activities make it a season worth experiencing.

For winter sports enthusiasts, Oslo offers excellent opportunities for skiing, snowboarding, and ice-skating. Just a short distance from the city, you'll find a variety of ski resorts and outdoor ice rinks where you can indulge in adrenaline-pumping adventures or glide gracefully on the ice.

The holiday season in Oslo is a special time, as the city becomes adorned with sparkling Christmas lights and decorations. Traditional Norwegian Christmas markets, such as the Christmas Fair at the Folk Museum, offer a chance to immerse yourself in the enchanting atmosphere and find unique gifts and crafts.

Winter markets are a treat for food lovers, with stalls selling warm, comforting delicacies like mulled wine, gingerbread cookies, and roasted chestnuts. Traditional Norwegian

Christmas dishes, such as lutefisk and rakfisk, can also be savored during this time.

Visiting Oslo's museums and indoor attractions is a great way to escape the cold while still experiencing the city's rich culture. From the National Museum of Art, Architecture and Design to the Oslo Opera House, there are plenty of cultural sites to explore and appreciate.

In conclusion, Oslo's distinct seasons offer diverse experiences throughout the year. Whether you choose to visit in the blooming spring, vibrant summer, colorful autumn, or enchanting winter, you'll find a unique charm and a range of activities and attractions that showcase the best of this Scandinavian capital.

2.2 Visa and Travel Requirements

Before traveling to Oslo, it's essential to ensure you have the necessary visa and travel requirements in order. Here are some key points to consider:

Visa Requirements:

Check the visa requirements for Norway based on your citizenship. Determine whether you need a Schengen visa, as Norway is part of the Schengen Area, allowing entry into multiple European countries, including Norway.

Research the specific visa category that applies to your purpose of travel, such as tourism, business, or study. Ensure that you meet all the requirements for that particular visa category.

Start the visa application process well in advance of your intended travel dates. The processing time for visas may vary, so it is advisable to apply as early as possible.

Gather all the necessary documents required for the visa application, such as a valid passport, completed application form, passport-sized photographs, travel itinerary, proof of accommodation in Oslo, proof of sufficient funds to cover your stay, travel insurance, and any additional documents specific to your visa category.

Submit the visa application to the nearest Norwegian embassy or consulate in your home country or the country where you are a legal resident. Follow the guidelines provided by the embassy or consulate regarding the submission process, fees, and required documents.

Track the status of your visa application online or through the embassy/consulate. Once your visa is approved, collect your passport with the visa stamp before your departure.

Valid Passport:

Ensure that your passport is valid for at least six months beyond your intended stay in Oslo. Some countries require a specific period of validity beyond the intended departure date, so check the passport validity requirements for your country of citizenship.

If your passport is approaching its expiration date or does not meet the validity requirements, renew it before applying for the visa. Contact your country's passport issuing authority or embassy/consulate for the renewal process and necessary documentation.

Keep a copy of your passport's biodata page separately from the original passport. It can be helpful in case of loss or theft.

Travel Insurance:

It is highly recommended to have travel insurance that provides coverage for medical expenses, trip cancellation or interruption, and loss or theft of personal belongings.

Research different travel insurance options and compare their coverage, including emergency medical treatment, evacuation, repatriation, and coverage for pre-existing medical conditions.

Read the insurance policy carefully to understand the terms, conditions, coverage limits, and exclusions. Ensure that the policy covers your entire stay in Oslo and any other destinations you plan to visit during your trip.

Carry a copy of your travel insurance policy and emergency contact information with you during your journey. It is also advisable to share the policy details with a trusted family member or friend.

Health Precautions:

Check for any health advisories or warnings issued for travelers visiting Norway. Stay updated with the latest information regarding COVID-19 travel restrictions, testing requirements, and quarantine protocols. Visit the official websites of the Norwegian government and the World Health Organization (WHO) for reliable and up-to-date information.

Consult your healthcare provider or visit a travel clinic well in advance of your trip to get personalized advice and recommendations based on your health history, destination, and planned activities.

Ensure that you are up to date with routine vaccinations and consider getting any additional vaccinations recommended for travel to Norway. Common vaccines may include measles-mumps-rubella (MMR), diphtheria-tetanus-pertussis, varicella (chickenpox), and influenza.

If you require prescription medications, ensure that you have an adequate supply for the duration of your stay in Oslo. Carry the medications in their original packaging, along with a copy of the prescription and a doctor's note if necessary.

Pack a basic travel health kit that includes essential items such as over-the-counter medications (pain relievers, antidiarrheals, antihistamines), adhesive bandages, antiseptic wipes, sunscreen, insect repellent, and any personal medical supplies you may need.

By following these guidelines and taking care of the necessary visa and travel requirements, you will be well-prepared for your trip to Oslo and can focus on enjoying the city's attractions, culture, and experiences. Remember to plan and complete these tasks well in advance to avoid any last-minute complications or delays.

2.3 Getting to Oslo

Oslo, the vibrant capital of Norway, is well-connected and easily accessible by various modes of transportation. Whether you prefer air travel, train journeys, or exploring the roads by car, there are several options to reach this captivating city.

By Air:

Oslo Airport, Gardermoen (OSL) serves as the main international gateway to Oslo. Located approximately 48 kilometers north of the city center, it is one of the busiest airports in the Nordic region. Numerous airlines operate regular flights to and from Oslo, connecting it to major cities worldwide.

Upon arrival at Oslo Airport, you have multiple transportation options to reach the city center. The most convenient and time-efficient option is the Airport Express Train, also known as Flytoget. Departing every 10-20 minutes, this high-speed train takes approximately 20 minutes to reach Oslo Central Station (Oslo S), located in the heart of the city. The train offers comfortable seating, luggage storage facilities, and free Wi-Fi, ensuring a pleasant journey. Additionally, there are airport buses available that provide direct transportation to various locations in Oslo, including the city center, major hotels, and popular attractions. Taxis are also readily available outside the airport terminals, providing a convenient but slightly more expensive option for reaching the city.

By Train:

If you prefer a scenic and relaxed mode of transportation, traveling to Oslo by train is a fantastic option. The Oslo Central Station (Oslo S) serves as the primary railway hub, connecting Oslo to neighboring cities in Norway, as well as several European destinations.

Oslo enjoys excellent rail connections with major Scandinavian cities like Stockholm and Gothenburg in Sweden and Copenhagen in Denmark. Comfortable and modern trains operated by companies such as NSB, SJ, and DSB provide a comfortable and convenient travel experience. The journey from Stockholm to Oslo, for example, offers breathtaking views of serene lakes, dense forests, and picturesque landscapes.

Traveling by train not only allows you to admire the natural beauty of the region but also provides easy access to Oslo's city center. The Oslo Central Station is conveniently located in the heart of the city, making it a perfect starting point to explore the attractions and landmarks.

By Car:

For those who enjoy the freedom and flexibility of driving, reaching Oslo by car is a viable option. Norway has an extensive and well-maintained road network, offering scenic routes and the opportunity to discover the stunning Norwegian countryside.

To reach Oslo by car, you can take advantage of the well-connected highways that link the city to neighboring countries and cities. The E6 highway is the main north-south route that connects Oslo to cities in Sweden, such as Stockholm and Gothenburg. The E18 highway, on the other hand, connects Oslo to cities in the south, including Kristiansand and Stavanger.

When traveling by car to Oslo, it's essential to plan your route in advance and consider factors such as toll roads and parking. Norway operates an electronic toll collection system, so ensure you have the necessary information and equipment for payment. Keep in mind that parking in the city center can be limited and expensive. It's advisable to research parking options beforehand or consider parking in designated areas outside the city center and using public transportation to reach your destination.

Additionally, it's worth noting that Oslo has implemented measures to reduce traffic congestion and promote sustainable transportation. The city encourages the use of public transportation, cycling, and walking as eco-friendly alternatives to cars. Oslo's efficient public transportation system, including buses, trams, and the metro, provides convenient access to various parts of the city.

Below are various apps in Norway that can enable you book for transportation:

Uber: Uber is a widely used app for booking rides in cities across Norway. With Uber, you can request a private car or taxi service and track your driver's arrival. The app provides fare estimates, cashless payments, and the option to share your trip details with friends or family for added safety.

Ruter Reise: Ruter Reise is an official app for public transportation in Oslo and the surrounding areas. It provides real-time schedules, route planning, ticket purchasing, and updates on delays or disruptions. The app covers buses, trams, metro lines, ferries, and trains, making it a comprehensive tool for navigating public transportation in the region.

NSB: NSB (Norges Statsbaner) is the official app for train travel in Norway. It allows you to search for train routes, view schedules, purchase tickets, and access your digital tickets for a seamless journey. The app covers both local and long-distance train services, making it convenient for exploring various parts of the country.

Flytoget: Flytoget is the official app for the Airport Express Train (Flytoget) in Oslo. It provides information on train departures, ticket purchases, and real-time updates. The app is particularly useful for travelers going to and from Oslo Airport, Gardermoen, with its fast and direct train service.

Vy: Vy (formerly known as NSB) is a comprehensive transportation app that covers trains, buses, and boats in Norway. It allows you to plan your journeys, purchase tickets, and access real-time information. The app covers both local and long-distance travel, making it useful for exploring different regions of Norway.

Oslo City Bike: Oslo City Bike is an app specifically designed for the city's bike-sharing system. With this app, you can locate available bikes, unlock them, and pay for your bike rental. It provides real-time availability updates and information on bike stations, making it easy to navigate Oslo on two wheels.

Entur: Entur is a national travel planner app that covers all modes of public transportation in Norway. It allows you to plan trips, view schedules, purchase tickets, and receive real-time updates on any disruptions. The app covers buses, trains, trams, ferries, and more, making it a comprehensive tool for transportation across the country.

Widerøe: Widerøe is a regional airline in Norway that connects various destinations within the country. The

Widerøe app allows you to search for flights, book tickets, manage your reservations, and receive notifications about flight status and changes. It is a useful app for travelers looking to explore remote and scenic parts of Norway.

SAS Scandinavian Airlines: SAS Scandinavian Airlines is a major airline that operates domestic and international flights in Norway. Their app provides a seamless booking experience, flight status updates, mobile check-in, and access to your boarding pass. It is a convenient tool for managing your flights when traveling to or within Norway.

Fjord Tours: Fjord Tours is an app that specializes in booking tours and transportation for exploring the stunning fjords of Norway. The app offers various package deals, including train and boat journeys, guided tours, and sightseeing adventures. It is a great app for travelers looking to experience the natural beauty of Norway's fjords.

In conclusion, Oslo offers multiple transportation options to suit different preferences and travel styles. Whether you choose to fly, take a scenic train journey, or explore the roads by car, reaching Oslo is convenient and accessible. Consider factors such as travel time, cost, and sustainability when selecting your preferred mode of transportation. Regardless of how you arrive, prepare to be captivated by the beauty, culture, and vibrant atmosphere of this remarkable Scandinavian city.

2.4 Transportation within Oslo

Oslo has a reliable and efficient public transportation system that makes it easy to explore the city and its surroundings. Here are the main modes of transportation within Oslo:

Public Trains and Metro:

Oslo boasts an extensive network of trains and metro lines that provide convenient transportation options for both residents and visitors. The metro system, known as the T-bane, is particularly efficient for navigating within the city center. With multiple lines and frequent service, you can easily reach major attractions, neighborhoods, and suburbs.

The T-bane is known for its reliability and punctuality, making it a popular choice for commuters and tourists alike. The metro stations are conveniently located throughout the city, allowing for seamless transfers and accessibility. Whether you're heading to the iconic Oslo Opera House, the vibrant Grünerløkka district, or the tranquil Frogner Park, the metro offers a convenient and efficient way to reach your destination.

Trains also play a crucial role in Oslo's public transportation system, connecting the city to its surrounding regions and neighboring cities. The local trains, operated by the Norwegian State Railways (NSB), provide a comfortable and scenic way to explore the outskirts of Oslo. You can embark on picturesque journeys to destinations like the charming coastal town of Drøbak or the idyllic lakeside village of Hønefoss.

Trams and Buses:

In addition to trains and the metro, Oslo's public transportation network includes trams and buses. Trams are a popular mode of transportation, especially for reaching popular areas and attractions within the city. They offer a convenient and nostalgic way to travel, allowing you to soak in the city's atmosphere as you glide through its streets. Tram routes cover key areas such as Aker Brygge, the waterfront district known for its vibrant dining and shopping scene, and Grünerløkka, a trendy neighborhood filled with hip cafés, boutiques, and parks.

Buses complement the tram and metro services, providing coverage to areas that may not be easily accessible by other modes of transportation. The bus routes are comprehensive and reach various neighborhoods and suburbs in Oslo. They are particularly useful for exploring residential areas, reaching hiking trailheads, or venturing to destinations outside the city center.

Oslo City Bike:

For those who prefer a more active and environmentally friendly mode of transportation, Oslo offers a convenient bike-sharing system called Oslo City Bike. With numerous bike stations strategically located throughout the city, you can easily rent a bike for short trips or leisurely rides. Cycling is a popular way to explore Oslo's neighborhoods, parks, and waterfront areas.

Renting an Oslo City Bike is simple and can be done through a mobile app or at designated bike stations. The bikes are well-maintained, equipped with adjustable seats and baskets for carrying personal belongings. It's a fantastic way to immerse yourself in the city's sights, enjoy the fresh air, and experience Oslo at your own pace.

Taxis and Rideshares:

If you prefer the convenience of door-to-door transportation or have specific needs, taxis and rideshare services are readily available in Oslo. Taxis can be found at designated taxi stands or hailed on the street. They provide a comfortable and reliable option for getting around the city, especially for longer journeys or when carrying heavy luggage.

Rideshare services like Uber also operate in Oslo, offering an alternative to traditional taxis. Using a smartphone app, you can easily request a ride, track your driver's location, and pay electronically. Rideshares can be a convenient option, particularly for shorter trips within the city.

It's important to note that while taxis and rideshares offer convenience, they can be more expensive compared to public transportation. It's advisable to check the fare estimates or compare prices between different services before selecting this mode of transportation.

In conclusion, Oslo provides a comprehensive and efficient public transportation system that caters to various needs and preferences. Whether you choose to travel by trains, metro, trams, buses, city bikes, taxis, or rideshares, you'll find that getting around Oslo is convenient, reliable, and offers opportunities to explore the city's diverse neighborhoods, attractions, and natural beauty

2.5 Accommodation Options

Oslo provides a range of accommodation options to suit various budgets and preferences. Here are some popular choices:

Oslo, as the capital of Norway and a popular tourist destination, offers a wide range of accommodation options to suit every traveler's needs and preferences. Whether you're looking for luxury, budget-friendly, unique, or alternative accommodations, Oslo has something for everyone.

Hotels:

Oslo features a diverse selection of hotels, ranging from luxurious five-star establishments to more affordable options. The majority of hotels are concentrated in the city center, placing you within easy reach of major attractions, restaurants, and transportation hubs. When choosing a hotel, it's advisable to research and compare options based on factors such as location, amenities, and guest reviews. This will help you find the accommodation that best matches your preferences and budget.

Boutique and Design Hotels:

For a unique and stylish experience, consider staying at one of Oslo's boutique or design hotels. These properties often boast contemporary architecture, trendy interiors, and personalized service. You'll find innovative design concepts, curated artwork, and attention to detail that create a distinct ambiance. Boutique and design hotels offer an opportunity to immerse yourself in the city's creative atmosphere and enjoy a memorable stay.

Hostels and Guesthouses:

If you're traveling on a budget or prefer a social atmosphere, hostels and guesthouses in Oslo are excellent options. These establishments provide affordable accommodations, often with dormitory-style rooms for budget-conscious travelers. Many hostels also offer private rooms for those seeking a bit more privacy. Hostels and guesthouses often have communal areas where travelers can meet, socialize, and share experiences. They are a great way to connect with fellow travelers and create lasting memories.

Apartment Rentals:

Renting an apartment or holiday home can be a convenient option, particularly for families, groups, or travelers seeking more space and the flexibility of self-catering. Numerous online platforms offer a variety of apartment rentals in Oslo, allowing you to choose a location that suits your preferences. Renting an apartment gives you the freedom to cook your meals, enjoy a home-like atmosphere, and experience the city from a local perspective.

Alternative Accommodations:

In addition to traditional hotels and apartments, Oslo also offers alternative accommodation options that provide a unique and memorable experience. Bed and breakfasts, eco-lodges, and houseboats are among the alternative accommodations available. Bed and breakfasts offer a more intimate and personalized stay, often serving homemade breakfasts and providing local insights. Eco-lodges provide eco-friendly accommodations that blend harmoniously with nature, allowing you to appreciate Oslo's natural beauty.

Houseboats offer a distinctive lodging experience, allowing you to stay on the water while enjoying the city's waterfront views.

Below are various apps you can use to book for accommodation in Norwy:

Booking.com: Booking.com is a popular app that allows you to search and book a wide range of accommodations, including hotels, apartments, guesthouses, and more. With a user-friendly interface and a vast selection of options, this app is a go-to choice for travelers seeking accommodation in Norway.

Airbnb: Airbnb is a renowned platform that connects travelers with unique accommodation options, such as private apartments, houses, and even traditional Norwegian cabins. The app enables you to browse listings, communicate with hosts, and book your desired accommodation conveniently.

Hotels.com: Hotels.com offers a comprehensive selection of hotels, resorts, and other types of accommodation throughout Norway. The app provides detailed information, including photos, reviews, and prices, allowing you to compare options and make informed decisions.

Expedia: Expedia is a popular travel booking platform that covers various aspects of your trip, including flights, hotels, and car rentals. The app provides a wide range of accommodation options in Norway, along with user reviews, flexible search filters, and competitive pricing.

HomeAway: HomeAway specializes in vacation rentals and offers a wide array of properties in Norway, including cozy cottages, waterfront homes, and spacious villas. The app allows you to explore unique and private accommodation options for a memorable stay in Norway.

Hostelworld: If you're looking for budget-friendly accommodations or a social atmosphere, Hostelworld is a go-to app for booking hostels in Norway. The app provides an extensive database of hostels, enabling you to compare prices, read reviews, and book dormitory beds or private rooms.

Nordic Choice Hotels: Nordic Choice Hotels is a well-known hotel chain in Norway. Their app allows you to search and book rooms in their properties, which include a variety of hotel brands and locations across the country. The app also provides loyalty rewards for frequent guests.

Trip.com: Trip.com is a comprehensive travel app that offers various services, including accommodation booking. It provides a wide range of options in Norway, from budget to luxury, and offers competitive prices and discounts.

Radisson Hotels: Radisson Hotels is a renowned international hotel brand with multiple properties in Norway. Their app allows you to browse and book rooms in their hotels, providing a seamless booking experience and access to exclusive offers.

HRS - Hotel Reservation Service: HRS is a popular app for booking hotels worldwide, including in Norway. The app offers a wide range of accommodation options and provides detailed information, including real-time availability, rates, and customer reviews.

Remember to read reviews, compare prices, and consider location and amenities when using these apps to book your accommodation in Norway.

When choosing accommodation in Oslo, it's important to consider factors such as proximity to attractions, public transportation access, amenities, and overall value for money. Oslo's popularity as a tourist destination means that booking in advance is advisable, especially during peak travel seasons. By selecting the accommodation that aligns with your preferences and budget, you'll enhance your stay in Oslo and create lasting memories of your visit to this captivating city.

CHAPTER THREE

Exploring Oslo's Neighborhoods

3.1. City Center:

Oslo's City Center is the heart of the Norwegian capital, bustling with activity, history, and modern attractions. Here, visitors can experience the perfect blend of old-world charm and contemporary urban lifestyle. The City Center is characterized by its wide streets, beautiful architecture, and a vibrant atmosphere that draws both locals and tourists alike.

Key attractions in the City Center include:

The Royal Palace: The Royal Palace, or Slottet, is a captivating architectural gem located at the end of Karl Johans Gate. As the official residence of the Norwegian monarch, it stands as a symbol of the country's monarchy and rich history. The palace's grand façade and beautifully manicured gardens offer a regal welcome to visitors. One of the highlights for tourists is the daily Changing of the Guard ceremony, where uniformed soldiers march with precision and exchange posts in an elaborate display of tradition and pomp. Visitors can witness this captivating event and marvel at the synchronized movements of the guards. The surrounding Palace Park provides a tranquil retreat, inviting visitors to relax, explore the well-maintained green spaces, and enjoy the peaceful ambiance.

Karl Johans Gate: As the main street of Oslo, Karl Johans Gate serves as a vibrant hub of activity and an essential thoroughfare in the city center. Stretching from the Royal Palace to the Central Station, it offers a delightful blend of history, culture, and commerce. Lined with an array of shops, boutiques, restaurants, and cafes, it presents endless opportunities for shopping, dining, and people-watching. Visitors can indulge in retail therapy, browsing through a variety of stores that cater to all tastes and budgets. From fashion boutiques and design shops to specialty stores and souvenir shops, Karl Johans Gate has something for everyone. Along the street, you'll also encounter significant cultural landmarks such as the Stortinget (the Norwegian Parliament) and the University of Oslo, adding a sense of intellectual and historical charm to the bustling atmosphere. A leisurely stroll along Karl Johans Gate is a must-do activity, allowing visitors to absorb the energy of the city, witness street performances, and take in the architectural splendor that lines the street.

Oslo Cathedral: Located on Stortorvet Square, Oslo Cathedral, or Oslo Domkirke, is a striking neo-Gothic church that dates back to the 17th century. The cathedral's imposing exterior and intricate architectural details are a testament to its historical and cultural significance. Step inside to discover its grand interior, adorned with beautiful stained glass windows, ornate decorations, and a tranquil ambiance. Oslo Cathedral is not only a place of worship but also a venue for cultural events and concerts. Visitors can attend religious services, enjoy the soul-stirring acoustics during musical performances, or marvel at the stunning architecture during special events. The cathedral's serene atmosphere invites contemplation and reflection, providing a peaceful respite from the bustling city center.

National Theatre: Recognized for its striking architecture, the National Theatre is a cultural icon in Oslo. Located near Karl Johans Gate, this renowned institution hosts a variety of artistic performances, including plays, ballets, operas, and musicals. The National Theatre serves as a platform for showcasing the works of Norwegian playwrights as well as international productions, attracting both local theater enthusiasts and international visitors. The theater complex comprises multiple auditoriums, each designed to provide an immersive and memorable experience. Visitors can indulge in a night of culture, witnessing captivating performances that range from classic dramas to contemporary works. The National Theatre is also home to a restaurant and café, where visitors can savor a pre-show dinner or enjoy a post-performance drink while discussing the artistic wonders they have just experienced.

These key attractions in Oslo's City Center represent the city's historical, cultural, and artistic heritage. The Royal Palace, Karl Johans Gate, Oslo Cathedral, and the National Theatre collectively offer a diverse range of experiences, allowing visitors to immerse themselves in Norwegian traditions, appreciate architectural marvels, indulge in shopping and dining, and engage with the vibrant cultural scene of the capital.

3.2. Grünerløkka:

Grünerløkka is a vibrant and trendy neighborhood located on the east side of the Akerselva River. Once an industrial district, it has transformed into a hip area known for its artistic flair, vintage shops, lively nightlife, and cozy cafes.

Highlights of Grünerløkka include:

Markveien: Nestled in Grünerløkka, Markveien is a vibrant and eclectic street that beckons shoppers with its unique offerings. It is a haven for those seeking vintage clothing, designer boutiques, and local handicrafts. As you wander along Markveien, you'll be greeted by a charming mix of trendy stores, independent shops, and hidden gems waiting to be discovered. Whether you're searching for a vintage treasure, a one-of-a-kind piece from a local designer, or simply want to soak up the neighborhood's creative vibes, Markveien offers an enticing shopping experience that caters to all tastes and styles. The street's dynamic atmosphere, colorful storefronts, and bustling energy make it a must-visit destination in Grünerløkka.

Grünerhagen: Situated in the heart of Grünerløkka, Grünerhagen is a picturesque park that provides a tranquil retreat from the urban bustle. This charming green oasis invites locals and visitors alike to relax, unwind, and enjoy nature's beauty. With its lush lawns, well-manicured flowerbeds, and tall trees providing shade, Grünerhagen is an idyllic spot for a leisurely stroll, a peaceful picnic, or simply a moment of respite. During the summer months, the park comes alive with laughter, as locals gather to bask in the sunshine, read a book, or engage in leisurely conversations. It's a wonderful place to immerse yourself in the laid-back atmosphere of Grünerløkka and soak up the neighborhood's charm.

Mathallen Oslo: For food enthusiasts, Mathallen Oslo is a culinary paradise that showcases the finest offerings from the Norwegian and international gastronomic scene. This vibrant food hall boasts a diverse range of stalls and vendors, each offering their own delectable specialties. From fresh seafood and mouthwatering meats to artisanal cheeses, gourmet chocolates, and exotic spices, Mathallen Oslo tantalizes the taste buds with its diverse array of flavors. Visitors can explore the various food stalls, interact with passionate food artisans, and indulge in a gastronomic journey that celebrates the best of Norwegian cuisine as well as global culinary traditions. Whether you're looking to sample traditional Norwegian dishes or embark on a culinary adventure around the world, Mathallen Oslo is a must-visit destination for food lovers.

Blå: Known as one of Oslo's most iconic music venues, Blå holds a special place in the city's vibrant music and cultural scene. Housed in a converted factory, Blå offers an alternative and edgy atmosphere that attracts music enthusiasts and nightlife lovers alike. The venue hosts an impressive lineup of live concerts, DJ sets, and cultural events spanning various genres and styles. Whether you're a fan of indie rock, electronic music, jazz, or experimental sounds, Blå offers a diverse program that caters to a wide range of musical tastes. With its riverside location along the Akerselva River, Blå provides a unique setting where visitors can enjoy captivating performances while taking in scenic views. It's a place where artists and audiences come together to celebrate the power of music, creating unforgettable experiences and forging lasting memories.

3.3. Frogner:

Frogner is an elegant and upscale neighborhood in Oslo, renowned for its leafy streets, exclusive residences, and cultural attractions. The centerpiece of Frogner is Frogner Park, home to the famous Vigeland Sculpture Park.

Key features of Frogner include:

Vigeland Sculpture Park: Considered a true masterpiece, Vigeland Sculpture Park stands as a testament to the artistic vision of Gustav Vigeland. As the largest sculpture park created by a single artist, it showcases over 200 sculptures that captivate visitors with their beauty, symbolism, and emotional depth. Among the park's highlights is the Monolith, an awe-inspiring column carved from a single granite block, featuring intricately intertwined human figures. The Wheel of Life, another prominent sculpture, depicts the cycle of human existence through its intricate design. One cannot miss the mischievous Angry Boy, an iconic bronze statue that has become a beloved symbol of the park. Vigeland Sculpture Park offers a profound artistic experience, inviting visitors to contemplate the human form, relationships, and the universal themes depicted in Vigeland's sculptures. Beyond the art, the park's expansive green spaces, serene ponds, and tree-lined pathways create a tranquil setting for a leisurely stroll, a family picnic, or simply a moment of reflection amidst the harmonious blend of art and nature.

Frogner Park: As a part of Vigeland Sculpture Park, Frogner Park adds another layer of natural beauty to the experience. This expansive park offers more than just sculptures; it boasts vast green lawns, meandering pathways, and beautiful flower gardens that burst with color during the warmer months. It's a haven for nature lovers, providing a peaceful retreat from the urban hustle and bustle. Visitors can take a leisurely walk, breathe in the fresh air, and revel in the serene ambiance created by the park's natural elements. The well-maintained gardens, with their meticulously arranged flowerbeds, offer a visual feast for the eyes and a place to relax amidst the tranquil beauty of nature. Frogner Park's combination of art, green spaces, and meticulously designed landscapes make it an enchating destination for both locals and tourists.

Frogner Village: Adjacent to Frogner Park, Frogner Village is a delightful neighborhood that exudes charm and elegance. With its quaint streets, tree-lined avenues, and beautifully preserved buildings, it offers a glimpse into Oslo's affluent residential areas. The village is known for its boutique shops, upscale restaurants, and cozy cafés, making it an ideal spot for a leisurely afternoon stroll. Visitors can meander through the streets, browsing the specialty stores that offer unique fashion finds, designer accessories, and stylish home decor. Frogner Village's dining scene is equally enticing, with a variety of upscale restaurants serving exquisite cuisine from around the world. From delectable seafood dishes to international flavors and local delicacies, the neighborhood caters to discerning palates seeking a culinary adventure. Frogner Village provides a refined and sophisticated atmosphere, allowing visitors to immerse themselves in Oslo's upscale lifestyle while exploring its charming streets and enjoying the local offerings.

3.4. Majorstuen:

Majorstuen is a vibrant and diverse neighborhood situated in the western part of Oslo. Known for its bustling streets and multicultural atmosphere, it offers a mix of shopping, dining, and cultural experiences.

Highlights of Majorstuen include:

Bogstadveien: Located in the bustling neighborhood of Majorstuen, Bogstadveien is a vibrant shopping street that attracts locals and tourists alike. As one of Oslo's most popular shopping destinations, it offers a diverse range of boutiques, department stores, and specialty shops. Fashion enthusiasts will find a plethora of options, from well-known international brands to local designers, ensuring that every style and taste is catered to. Beyond fashion, Bogstadveien also presents a treasure trove of home decor stores, where visitors can discover unique pieces to enhance their living spaces. Additionally, foodies will delight in the assortment of local delicacies available, from artisanal chocolates to gourmet treats. Bogstadveien's lively atmosphere, combined with its wide selection of shops, makes it an ideal destination for a memorable shopping experience.

Frogner Park and Bygdøy Peninsula: Majorstuen's proximity to Frogner Park and the beautiful Bygdøy Peninsula provides visitors with a wealth of cultural and natural attractions to explore. Frogner Park, also known as Vigeland Park, is a captivating outdoor gallery that showcases the works of renowned sculptor Gustav Vigeland. Within the park, visitors can marvel at the impressive collection of over 200 sculptures, depicting various human emotions and relationships. The park's serene pathways, lush gardens, and expansive lawns also provide a tranquil setting for leisurely walks, picnics, or simply enjoying the beauty of nature.

Just a short distance from Majorstuen lies the Bygdøy Peninsula, a picturesque area renowned for its cultural and historical significance. Bygdøy is home to several of Oslo's most popular museums, including the Viking Ship Museum, where visitors can marvel at remarkably preserved Viking ships and artifacts. The Fram Museum offers a fascinating exploration of polar exploration history, showcasing the polar exploration vessel Fram. In addition, the Kon-Tiki Museum invites visitors to learn about the intrepid adventures of Thor Heyerdahl and his expeditions across the oceans. Bygdøy Peninsula's combination of museums, scenic coastal views, and recreational areas make it a must-visit destination for history buffs, nature lovers, and those seeking to delve into Oslo's rich heritage.

Cafés and Restaurants: Majorstuen boasts a vibrant culinary scene, making it a true delight for food enthusiasts. Visitors can discover a diverse array of international cuisine alongside traditional Norwegian fare in the neighborhood's numerous cafés and restaurants. Start your day with a leisurely brunch, savoring freshly brewed coffee and mouthwatering pastries in one of the cozy cafés. Explore the streets of Majorstuen and find hidden gems offering flavors from around the world, including Asian, Mediterranean, Middle Eastern, and more. For those seeking a gourmet experience, the neighborhood also features upscale restaurants that combine exquisite ingredients, innovative techniques, and culinary artistry to create unforgettable dining experiences. Majorstuen's culinary offerings cater to all tastes and preferences, ensuring that visitors can indulge in a wide range of culinary delights and embark on a gastronomic journey during their stay in Oslo

3.5. Aker Brygge:

Aker Brygge is a vibrant waterfront district in Oslo, known for its modern architecture, lively atmosphere, and stunning views of the Oslo Fjord. Once an industrial area, it has been transformed into a thriving urban waterfront destination.

Key attractions and activities in Aker Brygge include:

The Oslo Fjord Promenade: Aker Brygge serves as the ideal starting point for a leisurely stroll along the Oslo Fjord Promenade. This scenic promenade offers panoramic views of the shimmering waters and the majestic surrounding landscape. As visitors walk along the promenade, they can take in the picturesque sights, including charming waterfront cafes where they can relax and soak up the maritime atmosphere. For those seeking a more immersive experience, boat tours are available, allowing travelers to explore the nearby islands and experience the fjord's beauty from a different perspective. Whether enjoying a cup of coffee by the water, admiring the passing boats, or embarking on a boat adventure, the Oslo Fjord Promenade promises an enchanting journey along one of Oslo's most captivating natural features.

Tjuvholmen: Connected to Aker Brygge by a footbridge, Tjuvholmen is a contemporary neighborhood that seamlessly blends art, gastronomy, and modern architecture. This vibrant area is renowned for its modern art galleries, where visitors can explore thought-provoking exhibitions and marvel at a diverse range of contemporary artworks. The Astrup Fearnley Museum, located in Tjuvholmen, is a highlight for art enthusiasts, offering a collection that showcases international contemporary art. Beyond the art scene, Tjuvholmen also boasts upscale restaurants that provide exquisite dining experiences with stunning waterfront views. From international cuisine to local delicacies, the neighborhood's gastronomic offerings cater to discerning palates. Trendy bars and lounges also dot the area, offering a vibrant nightlife scene. Tjuvholmen invites visitors to immerse themselves in the fusion of art, culinary delights, and modern urban charm.

Shopping and Entertainment: Aker Brygge is a shopper's paradise, with a wide range of fashion boutiques, design stores, and specialty shops that cater to various tastes and preferences. From renowned international brands to local designers, visitors can find an array of fashion-forward clothing, accessories, and unique souvenirs. The shopping experience at Aker Brygge is enhanced by the neighborhood's modern and stylish architecture, creating a visually appealing atmosphere as shoppers peruse the various stores. For entertainment seekers, Aker Brygge offers a modern cinema complex where movie enthusiasts can catch the latest releases in comfortable theaters. Additionally, the area is home to vibrant entertainment venues that host live music performances, theatrical shows, and cultural events, ensuring that visitors can immerse themselves in Oslo's dynamic arts and entertainment scene.

Outdoor Dining and Seafood: Aker Brygge is renowned for its outstanding seafood restaurants and inviting waterfront dining options. Visitors can indulge in a culinary journey that celebrates the freshest catches from the sea, including mouthwatering fish dishes, succulent shellfish, and traditional Norwegian specialties. The restaurants' picturesque locations along the harbor provide an idyllic setting to savor these delectable flavors while admiring the view of passing boats and the charming waterfront ambiance. Beyond seafood, Aker Brygge's dining scene offers a diverse range of international cuisine, ensuring that every palate is catered to. Whether enjoying a leisurely lunch, a romantic dinner, or simply a refreshing drink by the water, Aker Brygge's outdoor dining establishments promise a memorable gastronomic experience in a delightful coastal setting.

CHAPTER FOUR

Top Attractions in Oslo

4.1. The Royal Palace

The Royal Palace in Oslo is a grand testament to Norway's monarchy and a captivating attraction for visitors. Situated in the heart of the city, this iconic landmark serves as the official residence of the Norwegian monarch and has played a significant role in the country's history.

Built in the early 19th century, the Royal Palace is a prime example of neoclassical architecture, characterized by its elegant lines, symmetry, and ornate detailing. The exterior of the palace boasts a stately presence with its white façade, imposing columns, and regal statues. The surrounding gardens and parklands further enhance its beauty, providing a serene oasis amidst the bustling city.

A visit to the Royal Palace offers a glimpse into the opulent world of Norwegian royalty. Guided tours provide access to carefully curated sections of the palace, allowing visitors to explore its richly adorned rooms and halls. The King and Queen's chambers exude a sense of regality, with their lavish furnishings, intricate tapestries, and precious artwork. The banquet halls impress with their grandeur, capable of hosting state dinners and prestigious events.

The Royal Chapel within the palace is a place of both historical and spiritual significance. Adorned with exquisite stained glass windows, intricate woodwork, and beautiful altarpieces, it showcases the strong connection between the royal family and the Norwegian Church.

One of the highlights of a visit to the Royal Palace is witnessing the daily changing of the guard ceremony. This long-standing tradition attracts crowds of locals and tourists alike. Clad in their traditional uniforms, the guards parade in precise formations, creating a spectacle that adds a touch of pomp and ceremony to the palace grounds.

Beyond its architectural splendor and historical significance, the Royal Palace is a place that reflects the cultural identity and values of Norway. It serves as a symbol of the monarchy's connection with the people, offering glimpses into the lives of the royal family and providing a sense of national pride.

Whether it's admiring the exterior facade, strolling through the manicured gardens, exploring the luxurious interiors, or witnessing the changing of the guard, a visit to the Royal Palace in Oslo offers a captivating experience that immerses visitors in the grandeur and history of Norwegian royalty

4.2. Vigeland Park

Vigeland Park, located in the Frogner neighborhood of Oslo, is a captivating testament to the artistic mastery of Gustav Vigeland and a haven of beauty and contemplation. Spanning over 80 acres, this expansive sculpture park is a treasure trove of more than 200 bronze and granite sculptures, all meticulously crafted by Vigeland himself.

The highlight of Vigeland Park is undoubtedly the Monolith, a towering sculpture that commands attention with its sheer size and intricate design. Carved from a single block of granite, this awe-inspiring masterpiece reaches a height of 17 meters. The Monolith depicts a mesmerizing column of intertwined human figures, symbolizing the cycle of life, human connection, and the complexities of existence. The level of detail and the sense of movement within the sculpture evoke a range of emotions and provoke deep contemplation.

As visitors explore Vigeland Park, they encounter an array of other notable sculptures that showcase Vigeland's ability to capture the essence of human emotions and relationships. The Wheel of Life fountain, a striking circular structure adorned with numerous intertwined figures, represents the eternal cycle of life. The Bridge, adorned with intricately designed statues, depicts various stages and aspects of human existence, from childhood to old age, love to loss. Each sculpture tells a story, evoking empathy, introspection, and a profound sense of connection to the human experience.

The park's serene pathways, lined with beautifully maintained gardens and lush greenery, invite visitors to immerse themselves in a tranquil atmosphere. The carefully designed layout of the sculptures and the park's overall landscape harmonize to create a space that encourages reflection and appreciation of art and humanity. Visitors can take leisurely walks, find secluded spots for quiet contemplation, or simply sit and marvel at the skill and emotion captured within each sculpture.

Vigeland Park transcends its role as a mere collection of statues; it serves as a living testament to the universal themes of life, love, and human connection. The park's profound impact lies not only in the artistic brilliance of Vigeland's creations but also in its ability to evoke a range of emotions and provoke deep introspection. A visit to Vigeland Park is an enriching experience that invites visitors to engage with art, nature, and the complex nature of the human spirit

4.3. Oslo Opera House

The Oslo Opera House stands as a shining example of architectural brilliance and cultural significance, captivating art and culture enthusiasts from around the world. Situated on the picturesque waterfront, this modern marvel seamlessly blends contemporary design with traditional Norwegian craftsmanship.

The exterior of the opera house is a sight to behold. Designed to resemble an iceberg emerging from the sea, its sleek lines, white marble façade, and expansive glass windows create a striking visual impact. The most distinctive feature of the building is its slanted roof, which doubles as a public space accessible to visitors. As you ascend the roof, you are treated to panoramic views of the city skyline, the sparkling Oslofjord, and the surrounding natural beauty. This unique vantage point offers a fresh perspective on Oslo and serves as a popular gathering spot for locals and tourists alike.

Stepping inside the Oslo Opera House, you enter a world of artistic grandeur. The interior spaces are equally impressive, with state-of-the-art performance halls and rehearsal spaces that have been meticulously designed to provide optimal acoustics and visual experiences. The main auditorium, adorned with plush seating and adorned in warm tones, hosts world-class opera, ballet, and classical music performances that captivate audiences with their talent and artistry.

Beyond attending performances, visitors have the opportunity to explore the building's elegant interiors. The opera house features spacious lobbies, art galleries, and exhibition spaces, showcasing a diverse range of artistic expressions. From contemporary installations to historical artifacts, these spaces provide a glimpse into the rich cultural tapestry of Norway.

For those seeking a culinary experience, the Oslo Opera House houses a restaurant and a bar that offer delectable cuisine and refreshing beverages. Whether you're looking to indulge in a pre-show dinner or simply wish to savor the flavors while taking in the breathtaking surroundings, these dining options provide a perfect complement to the overall experience.

The Oslo Opera House stands as a vibrant cultural hub, inviting visitors to immerse themselves in the world of performing arts while reveling in its architectural splendor. It is a place where artistic expression, breathtaking views, and culinary delights converge, creating an unforgettable experience for all who step foot within its walls. Whether you come for a performance, to admire the design, or to simply soak in the atmosphere, the Oslo Opera House is a destination that embodies the essence of art, culture, and the spirit of Norway

4.4. Akershus Fortress

Perched on a hill overlooking Oslo's harbor, Akershus Fortress stands as a testament to Norway's fascinating history and serves as a cherished historic landmark. Dating back to the 13th century, this fortress has witnessed centuries of events and transformations, evolving from a medieval castle to a royal residence, a military stronghold, and now a hub of museums and cultural venues.

Stepping into Akershus Fortress, visitors are transported back in time, surrounded by walls that have withstood the test of centuries. Exploring the fortress's ramparts, towers, and dungeons offers a captivating glimpse into Norway's intriguing past. As you wander through the ancient corridors and climb the stone staircases, you can almost feel the echoes of the countless stories that have unfolded within these walls.

The medieval castle within the fortress provides insights into the country's rich history, shedding light on the lives of Norwegian nobility and the power struggles that shaped the nation. From grand halls adorned with medieval tapestries to well-preserved chambers that once housed royalty, the castle immerses visitors in the atmosphere of a bygone era.

Akershus Fortress is also home to the Norwegian Resistance Museum, a poignant tribute to the heroic efforts of Norwegians during World War II. Through immersive exhibits and artifacts, the museum tells the stories of the resistance movement, highlighting the courage and resilience of those who fought against the Nazi occupation. Visitors gain a deep appreciation for the sacrifices made and the unwavering spirit that characterized this dark chapter of Norwegian history.

Beyond its historical significance, Akershus Fortress offers breathtaking views of the Oslofjord and the surrounding cityscape. From its elevated position, visitors are treated to sweeping panoramas that capture the essence of Oslo's maritime charm. The expansive grounds surrounding the fortress provide a tranquil oasis amidst the bustling city, inviting leisurely walks, picnics, and even outdoor concerts during the summer months. It is a place where history and natural beauty intertwine, allowing visitors to immerse themselves in the captivating ambiance of the fortress and its surroundings.

Akershus Fortress stands as a testament to Norway's enduring spirit and rich heritage. It offers a multifaceted experience, where visitors can explore the echoes of the past, pay homage to the bravery of the resistance, and appreciate the stunning vistas that surround this historic landmark. Whether you come to delve into history, enjoy the views, or simply seek solace within its grounds, Akershus Fortress provides a captivating journey through time and an opportunity to connect with Norway's storied past.

4.5. The Viking Ship Museum

For a captivating exploration of Norway's Viking heritage, the Viking Ship Museum on the Bygdøy Peninsula stands as a must-visit destination. Stepping into this museum is like embarking on a journey back in time, immersing oneself in the world of the Vikings through their magnificent ships and the artifacts they left behind.

The highlight of the Viking Ship Museum is undoubtedly the three remarkably preserved Viking ships on display. The most famous among them is the Oseberg ship, a true marvel of craftsmanship and engineering. This well-preserved vessel, dating back to the 9th century, was excavated from a burial mound and stands as a testament to the Viking's mastery of shipbuilding. The Gokstad ship and the Tune ship, both equally impressive in their own right, provide further insight into the Viking's seafaring traditions and their advanced knowledge of maritime technology.

As visitors wander through the museum, they have the opportunity to marvel at these ancient ships up close, appreciating the intricate carvings, the impressive scale, and the sheer ingenuity that went into their construction. The ships themselves evoke a sense of wonder and curiosity, offering a tangible connection to a bygone era.

Beyond the awe-inspiring ships, the Viking Ship Museum houses a wealth of other artifacts and archaeological finds. Exhibits showcase a diverse range of objects that shed light on Viking culture and society. From intricately designed sledges and carriages to tools and weapons used in daily life, each artifact tells a story and provides a glimpse into the daily lives of the Vikings. The museum also displays skeletal remains found within burial mounds, offering valuable insights into Viking burial practices and beliefs.

The Viking Ship Museum goes beyond mere display; it provides a comprehensive experience for visitors to immerse themselves in the Viking Age. Guided tours offer in-depth knowledge and context, shedding light on the seafaring prowess of the Vikings, their trading networks, and their influence on Norwegian society. Interactive displays further engage visitors, allowing them to explore Viking history through engaging multimedia presentations and hands-on activities.

Another fascinating aspect of the Viking Ship Museum is the ongoing conservation work that takes place behind the scenes. Conservationists tirelessly work to preserve these delicate and irreplaceable artifacts, employing cutting-edge techniques and technologies. Visitors can witness firsthand the meticulous efforts undertaken to safeguard these treasures, ensuring their preservation for future generations.

The Viking Ship Museum stands as a testament to the Viking's enduring legacy and their significant impact on Norwegian history. It is a place where history comes alive, where visitors can marvel at the ancient ships, delve into Viking culture, and gain a deeper appreciation for the ingenuity and resilience of these seafaring explorers. A visit to the Viking Ship Museum is an immersive and enlightening experience, allowing one to connect with Norway's Viking past and gain a greater understanding of this remarkable civilization

4.6. Holmenkollen Ski Museum and Tower

Perched majestically on a hill overlooking Oslo, the Holmenkollen Ski Museum and Tower stands as a magnificent tribute to Norway's deep-rooted passion for winter sports and its illustrious skiing heritage. The iconic ski jump, a symbol of national pride since its establishment in 1892, has witnessed countless exhilarating ski jumping competitions and remains an integral part of Oslo's identity.

As visitors step into the Holmenkollen Ski Museum, they are transported into a world that celebrates the evolution of skiing throughout the ages. The museum's exhibits offer a captivating journey through time, showcasing the development of skiing equipment, techniques, and the sport's cultural significance. From ancient snowshoes and primitive wooden skis to the cutting-edge gear used in Olympic competitions, the museum paints a vivid picture of the sport's progression. Interactive displays invite visitors to immerse themselves in the ski culture, enabling them to try on traditional ski apparel, examine historical artifacts, and explore the impact of skiing on Norwegian society.

The Holmenkollen Ski Museum also invites visitors to experience the thrill of skiing through various engaging activities. Historical ski films provide a window into the past, transporting viewers to the early days of the sport when daring skiers conquered treacherous slopes. For those seeking a more hands-on experience, a ski simulator allows visitors to test their skills and feel the exhilaration of gliding down a virtual slope, even if they're not experienced skiers themselves.

However, a visit to the Holmenkollen Ski Museum and Tower would not be complete without ascending the iconic 60-meter tall tower. As visitors make their way to the observation deck, they are greeted with panoramic views that capture the essence of Oslo's breathtaking beauty. From this elevated vantage point, the city unfolds below, offering a bird's-eye view of the urban landscape, the shimmering waters of the Oslofjord, and the sprawling forests that surround the city. The awe-inspiring vista serves as a reminder of Norway's symbiotic relationship with nature and the profound connection between the Norwegian people and their stunning natural surroundings.

The Holmenkollen Ski Museum and Tower embodies Norway's enduring love affair with winter sports and its unwavering commitment to preserving its skiing heritage. It is a place where visitors can explore the fascinating history of skiing, engage with interactive exhibits, and bask in the breathtaking views from the tower. The museum stands as a testament to the indomitable spirit of Norwegian skiers and the unique blend of adventure, athleticism, and appreciation for nature that defines this remarkable nation.

These attractions in Oslo offer a diverse range of experiences, from exploring royal history and admiring captivating sculptures to delving into Viking culture and immersing oneself in the thrill of winter sports. Oslo truly showcases the best of Norway's cultural, historical, and natural wonders.

CHAPTER FIVE

Oslo's Cultural Delights

5.1. National Gallery:

The National Gallery in Oslo stands as a cultural treasure trove, beckoning art enthusiasts from around the world. With its impressive collection and diverse range of artworks, it offers a captivating journey through the history of Norwegian and international art.

As visitors step into the National Gallery, they are greeted by a vast array of masterpieces that showcase the evolution of artistic expression. One of the highlights of the gallery is the works of Edvard Munch, whose iconic paintings like "The Scream" and "Madonna" have become internationally recognized symbols of human emotion. These haunting and evocative pieces are sure to leave a lasting impression on anyone who encounters them.

Beyond Munch, the National Gallery boasts an extensive collection of renowned artists from different periods and styles. Visitors can immerse themselves in the genius of Vincent van Gogh, admiring his vibrant brushwork and emotional depth in pieces like "Self-Portrait with Straw Hat" and "Landscape with Snow." They can also marvel at the ethereal beauty of Claude Monet's impressionist landscapes or explore the bold and innovative creations of Pablo Picasso.

While the international artworks leave a profound impact, the National Gallery also takes great pride in showcasing the rich artistic heritage of Norway. The gallery's collection spans centuries, allowing visitors to trace the development of Norwegian art from the Romantic period to the present day. Paintings by renowned Norwegian artists such as Johan Christian Dahl, Harriet Backer, and Theodor Kittelsen provide insights into the country's cultural identity and its deep connection to nature.

The National Gallery's commitment to preserving and promoting Norwegian art extends beyond historical works. The gallery actively acquires and displays contemporary pieces, ensuring that visitors can engage with the latest trends and expressions in the Norwegian art scene. This dynamic approach allows visitors to witness the ongoing evolution of artistic practices in Norway and fosters a dialogue between the past and the present.

Moreover, the National Gallery serves as an educational hub, offering lectures, workshops, and guided tours to enhance visitors' understanding and appreciation of the artworks on display. Whether one is a seasoned art connoisseur or a curious novice, the gallery provides an inclusive and immersive environment that fosters a deep connection with the artistic heritage of Norway and the world.

In conclusion, the National Gallery in Oslo stands as a testament to the power of art to inspire, provoke, and transcend boundaries. Through its extensive collection of Norwegian and international artworks, it invites visitors on a captivating journey through various periods and styles. From the iconic masterpieces of Edvard Munch to the diverse range of artistic expressions on display, the National Gallery offers a comprehensive overview of artistic excellence and serves as a beacon for art enthusiasts seeking to enrich their cultural experiences.

5.2. Munch Museum:

Nestled in Oslo, the Munch Museum stands as a testament to the life and artistic genius of Edvard Munch, Norway's most celebrated artist. This museum offers visitors a captivating journey through the groundbreaking and emotionally charged art that defined Munch's career.

As visitors step into the Munch Museum, they are immediately immersed in an environment that reflects the artist's spirit and vision. The museum's collection is an extensive showcase of Munch's artworks, ranging from his iconic paintings and prints to sculptures and personal artifacts. This comprehensive representation allows visitors to explore the full breadth of Munch's creative output and gain a deeper understanding of his artistic process.

At the heart of the Munch Museum's collection are the seminal works that have become synonymous with Munch's name. Visitors can stand in awe of "The Dance of Life," a triptych that explores themes of love, desire, and mortality with its vibrant colors and dynamic composition. They can contemplate the raw emotions captured in "Puberty," a powerful depiction of adolescent uncertainty and awakening. And they can witness the haunting vulnerability in "The Sick Child," a work that reflects Munch's personal experiences with illness and loss.

Beyond these iconic pieces, the Munch Museum delves deeper into the artist's exploration of human emotions and existential angst. Visitors can encounter the despair and anguish in "The Scream," Munch's most famous work, which has become an enduring symbol of anxiety and existential dread. They can experience the intensity of passion and jealousy in "Vampire" and "Jealousy," where Munch delves into the darker aspects of human relationships. Each artwork serves as a window into Munch's inner world, inviting viewers to grapple with the complexities of the human condition.

Moreover, the Munch Museum provides a glimpse into Munch's creative process and the themes that permeated his oeuvre. Through the display of personal artifacts, sketchbooks, and letters, visitors can gain insights into the artist's inspirations, motivations, and struggles. This behind-the-scenes perspective adds depth to the viewing experience, allowing visitors to appreciate the immense dedication and artistic vision that drove Munch throughout his career.

The museum also strives to contextualize Munch's work within the broader artistic and historical movements of his time. Exhibitions and curated displays explore Munch's interactions with fellow artists, his engagement with the Symbolist and Expressionist movements, and his impact on the art world at large. This contextualization further enriches visitors' understanding of Munch's significance as an artist and his lasting influence on the development of modern art.

In conclusion, the Munch Museum is a haven for art enthusiasts and individuals seeking to engage with the profound and emotionally charged works of Edvard Munch.

Through its vast collection, the museum invites visitors on a journey of exploration, introspection, and self-reflection. By showcasing Munch's paintings, prints, sculptures, and personal artifacts, the museum sheds light on his creative process, his thematic preoccupations, and his enduring legacy. It is a place where visitors can immerse themselves in the artist's world, gaining a deeper understanding of human emotions, existential angst, and the power of art to evoke profound emotions and resonate across generations.

5.3. The Oslo Cathedral:

Nestled in Oslo, the Munch Museum stands as a testament to the life and artistic genius of Edvard Munch, Norway's most celebrated artist. This museum offers visitors a captivating journey through the groundbreaking and emotionally charged art that defined Munch's career.

As visitors step into the Munch Museum, they are immediately immersed in an environment that reflects the artist's spirit and vision. The museum's collection is an extensive showcase of Munch's artworks, ranging from his iconic paintings and prints to sculptures and personal artifacts. This comprehensive representation allows visitors to explore the full breadth of Munch's creative output and gain a deeper understanding of his artistic process.

At the heart of the Munch Museum's collection are the seminal works that have become synonymous with Munch's name. Visitors can stand in awe of "The Dance of Life," a triptych that explores themes of love, desire, and mortality with its vibrant colors and dynamic composition. They can contemplate the raw emotions captured in "Puberty," a powerful depiction of adolescent uncertainty and awakening. And they can witness the haunting vulnerability in "The Sick Child," a work that reflects Munch's personal experiences with illness and loss.

Beyond these iconic pieces, the Munch Museum delves deeper into the artist's exploration of human emotions and existential angst. Visitors can encounter the despair and anguish in "The Scream," Munch's most famous work, which has become an enduring symbol of anxiety and existential dread. They can experience the intensity of passion and jealousy in "Vampire" and "Jealousy," where Munch delves into the darker aspects of human relationships. Each artwork serves as a window into Munch's inner world, inviting viewers to grapple with the complexities of the human condition.

Moreover, the Munch Museum provides a glimpse into Munch's creative process and the themes that permeated his oeuvre. Through the display of personal artifacts, sketchbooks, and letters, visitors can gain insights into the artist's inspirations, motivations, and struggles. This behind-the-scenes perspective adds depth to the viewing experience, allowing visitors to appreciate the immense dedication and artistic vision that drove Munch throughout his career.

The museum also strives to contextualize Munch's work within the broader artistic and historical movements of his time. Exhibitions and curated displays explore Munch's interactions with fellow artists, his engagement with the Symbolist and Expressionist movements, and his impact on the art world at large. This contextualization further enriches visitors' understanding of Munch's significance as an artist and his lasting influence on the development of modern art.

In conclusion, the Munch Museum is a haven for art enthusiasts and individuals seeking to engage with the profound and emotionally charged works of Edvard Munch. Through its vast collection, the museum invites visitors on a journey of exploration, introspection, and self-reflection. By showcasing Munch's paintings, prints, sculptures, and personal artifacts, the museum sheds light on his creative process, his thematic preoccupations, and his enduring legacy. It is a place where visitors can immerse themselves in the artist's world, gaining a deeper understanding of human emotions, existential angst, and the power of art to evoke profound emotionLocated in the heart of Oslo, the Oslo Cathedral, also known as Oslo Domkirke or the Cathedral of St. Hallvard, stands as a prominent landmark and a testament to Norway's rich religious history. Constructed in the 17th century, this architectural gem showcases a captivating blend of Baroque and Neo-Gothic styles, capturing the attention of visitors with its awe-inspiring beauty.

Approaching the Oslo Cathedral, one is greeted by an exterior that exudes grandeur and timelessness. The facade's intricate details, ornate carvings, and soaring spires create a visual feast for the eyes, inviting onlookers to marvel at the craftsmanship and artistic mastery of the builders. This architectural fusion of Baroque and Neo-Gothic elements reflects the evolution of architectural styles throughout the cathedral's construction and renovation over the centuries.

Stepping through the cathedral's doors, visitors are greeted by a sanctuary that is nothing short of breathtaking. The interior of the Oslo Cathedral is a sanctuary of serenity and spiritual reflection. Sunlight streams through beautiful stained glass windows, casting vibrant hues and delicate patterns on the stone floors and walls. These meticulously crafted windows depict biblical scenes, saints, and other religious symbolism, adding to the ethereal ambiance of the space.

The cathedral's interior is adorned with intricate woodwork, ornate carvings, and finely detailed sculptures. The craftsmanship and attention to detail are evident in every nook and cranny, reflecting the dedication and skill of the artisans who contributed to the cathedral's construction and adornment. Magnificent vaulted ceilings soar overhead, creating an atmosphere of awe and reverence.

Beyond its architectural and artistic splendor, the Oslo Cathedral holds deep religious significance for the Diocese of Oslo. As the main church of the diocese, it serves as a spiritual center and a place of worship for the local community. The cathedral hosts important religious ceremonies, including royal coronations and weddings, adding a sense of regal history and tradition to its sacred walls.

Visiting the Oslo Cathedral offers more than just a visual feast and a glimpse into Norway's religious heritage. It provides an opportunity for visitors to pause, reflect, and experience a sense of tranquility amidst the bustling city. The cathedral's hallowed halls and spiritual atmosphere invite contemplation and reverence, allowing individuals to connect with their faith or find solace in the beauty of the surroundings.

In conclusion, the Oslo Cathedral stands as a remarkable testament to the architectural and religious heritage of Norway. With its blend of Baroque and Neo-Gothic styles, it captures the imagination of visitors and offers a glimpse into the country's religious past. The cathedral's interior, adorned with stunning stained glass windows, intricate woodwork, and vaulted ceilings, creates a sacred space for contemplation and worship. As the main church of the Diocese of Oslo, the cathedral holds great historical and cultural significance, hosting significant religious ceremonies throughout the years. A visit to the Oslo Cathedral is a chance to immerse oneself in the spirituality, architectural splendor, and peaceful ambiance of this remarkable places and resonate across generations.

5.4. Nobel Peace Center:

Nestled near the Oslo City Hall, the Nobel Peace Center stands as a beacon of inspiration and a thought-provoking museum dedicated to honoring the Nobel Peace Prize laureates and promoting dialogue on peace and human rights. This extraordinary center presents engaging exhibitions that highlight the remarkable achievements and enduring contributions of notable peace laureates from around the world, offering visitors a profound and transformative experience.

As visitors step into the Nobel Peace Center, they are immersed in a world that celebrates the individuals who have dedicated their lives to advancing peace and justice.

The exhibitions pay homage to the extraordinary accomplishments of laureates such as Martin Luther King Jr., Mother Teresa, and Malala Yousafzai, among many others. Each laureate's story is brought to life through a combination of artifacts, personal belongings, photographs, and compelling narratives, shedding light on their struggles, triumphs, and lasting impact on society.

The Nobel Peace Center leverages innovative and interactive displays to create an engaging and immersive experience for visitors. State-of-the-art multimedia presentations, including audiovisual installations, virtual reality experiences, and interactive touch screens, invite visitors to explore the laureates' journeys and immerse themselves in the stories that shaped their tireless pursuit of peace. Through these dynamic mediums, visitors gain a deeper understanding of the laureates' work, their philosophies, and the challenges they faced.

Moreover, the center's exhibitions inspire contemplation and dialogue about pressing global issues related to peace and human rights. Thoughtfully curated displays tackle a range of topics, including disarmament, conflict resolution, gender equality, and environmental sustainability. These exhibitions not only highlight the laureates' individual contributions but also encourage visitors to reflect on their own role in fostering peace and positive change within their communities and the world at large.

The Nobel Peace Center serves as a platform for engagement, encouraging visitors to actively participate in shaping a more peaceful and just future. Through workshops, discussions, and educational programs, the center fosters an environment that nurtures dialogue and collaboration. It provides a space where individuals from diverse backgrounds can come together to explore shared values, exchange perspectives, and work towards common goals of peace, equality, and social justice.

Beyond its exhibitions and programs, the Nobel Peace Center stands as a symbol of hope and inspiration. It honors the enduring legacy of the Nobel Peace Prize and its transformative impact on individuals and societies. The center's location near the Oslo City Hall, where the Nobel Peace Prize ceremony takes place annually, further underscores its significance as a hub for peacebuilding and a reminder of the power of individuals to make a difference.

In conclusion, the Nobel Peace Center is a remarkable institution that celebrates the achievements of Nobel Peace Prize laureates and fosters dialogue on peace, human rights, and social justice. Through engaging exhibitions, interactive displays, and immersive installations, the center invites visitors to reflect on the laureates' remarkable contributions and their own capacity to effect change. By inspiring contemplation, fostering dialogue, and providing a platform for engagement, the Nobel Peace Center empowers individuals to become catalysts for peace in their own lives and communities. It stands as a testament to the transformative power of individuals and serves as a constant reminder that peace is attainable through collective action and unwavering commitment

5.5. The Astrup Fearnley Museum of Modern Art:

Perched on the picturesque Tjuvholmen Peninsula, the Astrup Fearnley Museum of Modern Art stands as a beacon of contemporary art in Oslo, captivating visitors with its striking architecture and impressive collection. This renowned museum invites art enthusiasts and curious visitors to embark on a journey through the vibrant and ever-evolving world of contemporary art.

The Astrup Fearnley Museum boasts a diverse and thought-provoking collection of contemporary works from both established and emerging artists. The collection spans a wide range of mediums, including painting, sculpture, photography, and installation art, providing a multi-dimensional experience for visitors. The museum's curatorial vision embraces bold experimentation, pushing boundaries and challenging conventional notions of art.

Visitors to the Astrup Fearnley Museum are treated to a dynamic and engaging exhibition program that delves into social, cultural, and political themes of our time. Thoughtfully curated exhibitions present a kaleidoscope of perspectives, inviting viewers to contemplate the complexities of the modern world. Through the power of art, the museum sparks conversations, raises awareness, and encourages critical thinking about pressing issues and societal transformations.

The Astrup Fearnley Museum serves as a platform for both established artists who have already made their mark and emerging talents who are pushing the boundaries of artistic expression. It nurtures innovation and creativity, providing a space for artists to experiment, evolve, and challenge traditional norms. Visitors have the unique opportunity to witness the cutting-edge trends and diverse artistic expressions that define contemporary art.

Beyond its exceptional art collection and thought-provoking exhibitions, the museum's location on the waterfront of the Oslofjord adds an extra layer of allure to the overall experience. As visitors explore the museum's galleries, they are treated to panoramic views of the shimmering waters, creating a harmonious interplay between the artistic creations inside and the natural beauty outside. This serene setting enhances the contemplative atmosphere and offers a moment of respite, allowing visitors to immerse themselves fully in the art and the surroundings.

The Astrup Fearnley Museum is more than just a repository of art; it is a catalyst for dialogue, inspiration, and self-reflection. Through educational programs, workshops, and guided tours, the museum encourages active engagement and invites visitors to delve deeper into the artistic process and the broader cultural context. It fosters a vibrant community where individuals can connect, share ideas, and explore the transformative power of contemporary art.

In conclusion, the Astrup Fearnley Museum of Modern Art stands as a captivating testament to the vibrancy and diversity of contemporary art in Oslo. Its striking architecture, impressive collection, and thought-provoking exhibitions create an immersive experience that engages the senses and stimulates the mind. As visitors explore the museum's galleries and take in the breathtaking views of the

Oslofjord, they are transported to a world where artistic expression knows no boundaries. The Astrup Fearnley Museum serves as a cultural hub, inspiring dialogue, fostering creativity, and igniting a passion for contemporary art in all who cross its threshold.

CHAPTER SIX

Outdoor Adventures in Oslo

6.1. Oslo Fjord Boat Tours:

As you step aboard an Oslo Fjord boat tour, get ready to be immersed in the enchanting beauty of the landscapes that unfold along the fjord's shores. The calm waters create a serene atmosphere as the boat glides through the fjord, revealing a breathtaking tapestry of sights that will leave you in awe. Admire the charming waterfront houses that dot the shoreline, showcasing traditional Norwegian architecture and adding a touch of quaintness to the surroundings.

The fjord is adorned with idyllic islands, each with its own unique character and allure. As you sail past them, you'll be captivated by the picturesque scenery and the sense of tranquility they exude. The verdant hillsides that frame the fjord provide a stunning backdrop, creating a postcard-worthy view at every turn.

Throughout the tour, the knowledgeable guides on board will share captivating stories about the fjord's historical and cultural significance to Oslo. Learn about the fjord's role as a vital waterway for trade and transportation, dating back centuries. Discover how it shaped the development of the city, serving as a hub for maritime activities and contributing to Oslo's growth and prosperity.

One of the highlights of the Oslo Fjord boat tour is the opportunity to disembark at some of the islands that speckle the fjord. Hovedøya and Gressholmen are particularly popular destinations, offering a glimpse into the region's rich history. Explore the ancient ruins that stand as remnants of bygone eras, providing a tangible connection to Oslo's past. Take leisurely walks along the islands' trails, allowing you to fully appreciate the beauty of nature and discover hidden gems tucked away amidst the lush surroundings. Find a cozy spot for a picnic, where you can savor delicious treats amidst the serenity of the fjord.

Whether you choose to embark on a daytime excursion or opt for a magical sunset cruise, Oslo Fjord boat tours promise an unforgettable experience. The shifting hues of the sky reflecting on the tranquil waters create an ambiance that is both captivating and serene. Breathe in the fresh sea air as you take in the remarkable views and the sense of calm that envelops you. The memories you create during the boat tour, surrounded by the fjord's beauty and immersed in Oslo's maritime history, will stay with you long after the journey is over, serving as a cherished reminder of your time in this captivating Norwegian city

6.2. Bygdøy Peninsula and Beaches:

The Bygdøy Peninsula is a true gem for those seeking a blend of cultural immersion and natural beauty. Begin your exploration by immersing yourself in the fascinating world of the Vikings at the Viking Ship Museum. Marvel at the exquisitely preserved Viking longships, such as the Oseberg ship and the Gokstad ship, which have endured for over a thousand years. These magnificent vessels provide a glimpse into the seafaring prowess and craftsmanship of the Vikings, offering a unique window into Norway's rich maritime history.

Continue your journey through history at the Fram Museum, where you'll encounter the legendary polar exploration ship, Fram. Step aboard this well-preserved vessel and embark on a virtual journey to the polar regions. Learn about the courageous expeditions led by renowned explorers such as Fridtjof Nansen and Roald Amundsen, and gain a deeper appreciation for the challenges they faced in their quest for discovery. The museum's interactive exhibits and multimedia presentations bring their remarkable stories to life, leaving you in awe of their achievements.

Adjacent to the Fram Museum, the Kon-Tiki Museum celebrates the intrepid spirit of Thor Heyerdahl and his daring expeditions across the oceans. Discover the legendary Kon-Tiki raft, used by Heyerdahl to sail across the Pacific Ocean, as well as artifacts from his other voyages, including the Ra II and the Tigris. Gain insights into Heyerdahl's theories on ancient civilizations and his quest to prove that ancient mariners could have traveled great distances. The museum's engaging displays and informative exhibits showcase the adventurous spirit and scientific curiosity that defined Heyerdahl's explorations.

After immersing yourself in history and culture, take a leisurely stroll along the inviting beaches that grace the Bygdøy Peninsula. Huk Beach, with its pristine sandy shores, offers a perfect spot to soak up the sun and enjoy the gentle lapping of the fjord's waters. Take a refreshing dip in the clear waters or simply relax on the beach, savoring the peaceful ambiance and the stunning views of the surrounding landscape. Paradisbukta, another picturesque beach, invites you to unwind amidst nature's beauty, providing a serene escape from the urban hustle and bustle.

Bygdøy Peninsula seamlessly blends cultural experiences with seaside relaxation, making it a beloved destination for both locals and visitors. Whether you are an avid history enthusiast, a nature lover, or simply seeking a tranquil beach getaway, Bygdøy Peninsula offers an enchanting retreat. The harmonious coexistence of museums filled with captivating stories and inviting beaches brimming with natural beauty creates a captivating atmosphere that lures visitors back time and time again. Prepare to be immersed in the treasures of Bygdøy Peninsula, where cultural wonders and seaside bliss await your discovery.

6.3. Oslo's Forests and Nature Reserves:

For nature enthusiasts, Oslo's surrounding forests and nature reserves offer a haven of endless exploration and breathtaking beauty. Prepare to embark on an adventure through the vast wilderness of Nordmarka Forest, a pristine expanse of greenery that stretches as far as the eye can see. Lace up your hiking boots and set off on winding trails that lead you deeper into the heart of nature. As you traverse the forest, you'll discover hidden gems, from serene lakes like Sognsvann and Østmarksetra to picturesque picnic spots nestled among the trees. Cast your line into the crystal-clear waters and try your luck at fishing, or simply bask in the peaceful ambiance, surrounded by the sights and sounds of nature.

Oslo's forests are teeming with wildlife, offering excellent opportunities for spotting some of Norway's iconic creatures. Keep your eyes peeled for graceful deer gracefully meandering through the underbrush, mischievous foxes darting among the trees, and an array of bird species filling the air with their melodious songs. As you wander through the forests, you'll witness firsthand the harmonious ecosystem that thrives in this natural paradise.

For a unique nature experience within the city limits, visit the stunning botanical gardens at the University of Oslo. Stroll along the meticulously curated paths and marvel at the vibrant array of plant species from around the world. Take a moment to relax in the tranquil oasis, immersing yourself in the scents and colors of the garden's flora.

Another must-visit destination for nature lovers is Grefsenkollen, a popular viewpoint that offers panoramic vistas of Oslo and its surrounding natural landscapes. As you ascend to the top, the city's skyline gives way to sweeping views of sprawling forests, sparkling fjords, and majestic mountains. Breathe in the fresh mountain air and let the awe-inspiring scenery take your breath away. Grefsenkollen serves as a reminder of the close connection between Oslo's urban charm and the captivating nature that envelopes it.

Oslo's forests and nature reserves provide a haven for nature lovers seeking tranquility and a chance to reconnect with the great outdoors. Whether you are embarking on a leisurely hike, immersing yourself in the serenity of a tranquil lake, spotting wildlife in its natural habitat, exploring the diverse botanical wonders, or capturing breathtaking views from a panoramic viewpoint, Oslo's natural wonders offer an opportunity to escape the hustle and bustle of city life. Embrace the tranquility, find solace in the embrace of nature, and let the beauty of Oslo's forests and nature reserves captivate your senses

6.4. Skiing and Winter Activities:

When winter casts its magical spell over Oslo, transforming the city into a glistening wonderland, the ski resorts become the epicenter of excitement and adventure. Prepare to indulge in the snowy delights as you immerse yourself in Oslo's winter wonderland.

Holmenkollen, renowned as one of Norway's most iconic ski areas, beckons with its majestic slopes and thrilling activities. Strap on your skis and hit the downhill slopes, where you can challenge yourself with twists, turns, and thrilling descents. Feel the rush of adrenaline as you carve your way through the powdery snow, surrounded by breathtaking vistas. For those seeking an unforgettable experience, don't miss the opportunity to visit the world-famous Holmenkollen Ski Jump. Ascend to the top of the towering structure and marvel at the panoramic views of the city and the surrounding winter landscape. Imagine the courage of the athletes who soar through the air with grace and precision. If you're feeling adventurous, you can even try your hand at biathlon shooting, combining the skills of cross-country skiing and marksmanship in a thrilling winter sport.

Cross-country skiing enthusiasts will find themselves in paradise as numerous trails wind their way through Oslo's parks and forests. Glide gracefully through snow-covered landscapes, propelled by the rhythmic motion of your skis.

Feel the crisp winter air invigorate your senses as you traverse the pristine trails, surrounded by nature's tranquility. Whether you choose to explore the trails of Nordmarka Forest, Frognerseteren, or other picturesque locations, cross-country skiing in Oslo offers a serene and immersive winter experience.

For a truly unique winter adventure, consider joining a guided snowshoeing expedition. Strap on the lightweight snowshoes and venture into the snowy wilderness, where you'll traverse off-the-beaten-path trails, forging your way through the deep snow. With each step, you'll appreciate the untouched beauty of Oslo's winter landscapes, experiencing a sense of tranquility and connection with nature that is unparalleled.

If you're seeking a dash of thrill and exhilaration, embark on a dog sledding adventure. Feel the power and excitement as a team of eager huskies pulls you through the snowy terrain. Let the rhythmic sound of their paws on the snow create a symphony of winter enchantment as you glide across the frozen landscapes. Experience the bond between human and canine, and marvel at the teamwork and agility of these remarkable sled dogs.

Whether you're an experienced skier seeking new challenges or a first-timer eager to try your hand at winter sports, Oslo's winter activities cater to all levels of experience. From the adrenaline rush of downhill skiing and the serenity of cross-country trails to the thrill of snowshoeing and the magical allure of dog sledding, Oslo's winter wonderland offers a multitude of options to suit every taste and preference. Prepare to create unforgettable memories as you embrace the pristine beauty of Oslo's winter landscape and partake in the exhilarating adventures that await you

6.5. Cycling and Hiking Trails:

Oslo's cycling and hiking trails beckon adventurers to immerse themselves in the city's natural beauty while experiencing the unique fusion of urban and rural landscapes. Strap on your helmet and hop on a bicycle as you embark on a journey along the city's dedicated cycling paths, each offering its own distinctive charm. Pedal along the picturesque Akerselva River trail, where the tranquil waters guide you through a serene landscape adorned with lush greenery and historical landmarks. The soothing sound of flowing water accompanies your ride as you pass quaint neighborhoods, charming cafés, and vibrant street art that dots the path. Alternatively, explore the vibrant waterfront promenades, where the shimmering fjord provides a stunning backdrop as you glide past trendy restaurants, bustling markets, and lively marinas.

For a truly enchanting cycling experience, consider renting a bike and venturing into the peaceful oasis of Ekeberg Park. As you pedal through the park's rolling green hills, you'll encounter captivating art installations scattered amidst the natural landscape. Marvel at the harmonious blend of artistic expression and nature's beauty, with each sculpture and artwork adding a touch of intrigue and wonder to your journey. Take breaks to soak in the serene atmosphere, perhaps enjoying a picnic amidst the park's idyllic surroundings.

Hiking enthusiasts will find themselves spoiled for choice with Oslo's array of trails that showcase the city's panoramic views and natural wonders. Grefsenkollen and Vettakollen are two popular destinations that offer sweeping vistas of the city and its surrounding fjords. Embark on a rewarding hike as you ascend to these viewpoints, taking in the breathtaking scenery that unfolds before you. From the majestic fjords to the sprawling urban landscape, the views from these vantage points are nothing short of awe-inspiring.

For those seeking a more extensive adventure, consider tackling the renowned Oslo to Bergen hiking trail. This multi-day trek leads you through awe-inspiring mountainous terrain, enchanting valleys, and charming villages. Immerse yourself in the rugged beauty of Norway's wilderness as you navigate the winding trails that connect Oslo and Bergen. Along the way, discover hidden gems, encounter cascading waterfalls, and experience the tranquility of untouched nature.

Oslo's cycling and hiking trails offer boundless opportunities to connect with nature, embrace an active lifestyle, and uncover hidden treasures along the way. Whether you choose to pedal along the city's cycling paths, explore the art-filled landscapes of Ekeberg Park, hike to breathtaking viewpoints, or embark on a multi-day adventure, each journey promises an immersive experience that reveals the captivating essence of Oslo's natural and urban landscapes. So grab your bike or lace up your hiking boots, and let the trails of Oslo guide you on an unforgettable exploration of the city's hidden gems and breathtaking vistas

CHATER SEVEN

Oslo culinary scene

7.1. Traditional Norwegian Cuisine:

Norway boasts a rich culinary heritage rooted in its natural resources and traditional methods of food preparation. Traditional Norwegian cuisine is known for its emphasis on hearty and wholesome ingredients. Here are some iconic dishes you should try when exploring Oslo:

Fårikål:

Fårikål holds a special place in Norwegian culinary traditions and is often referred to as the national dish of Norway. This comforting stew is made by combining tender pieces of lamb with layers of cabbage, whole black peppercorns, and a touch of wheat flour to thicken the broth. The dish is prepared in a large pot, allowing the flavors to meld together slowly over low heat, resulting in a rich and hearty meal. Fårikål is traditionally enjoyed during the autumn months when the lambs have been grazing in the mountains, and it provides a warm and satisfying meal to ward off the chill of the season. The tender lamb, combined with the mild sweetness of the cabbage and the subtle heat from the black peppercorns, creates a harmonious blend of flavors that captures the essence of Norwegian comfort food.

Lutefisk:

Lutefisk is a distinctive dish that holds a significant place in Norwegian culinary heritage. It starts with dried and cured codfish that is soaked in a water and lye mixture, which softens the fish and gives it a unique gelatinous texture. The lye treatment also imparts a distinct flavor to the fish. After the soaking process, the lutefisk is thoroughly rinsed to remove the lye before it is cooked. Lutefisk is often served with boiled potatoes, peas, bacon, and a creamy white sauce to complement the delicate flavors of the fish. The dish is particularly popular during the Christmas season and is often enjoyed as part of the traditional Norwegian holiday feast. Lutefisk has a devoted following among Norwegians, and its preparation and consumption have become a cherished cultural tradition.

Rakfisk:

Rakfisk is a traditional Norwegian delicacy that showcases the country's affinity for preserved and fermented foods. This dish involves marinating freshwater trout or char in a mixture of salt and water for several months, allowing the fish to undergo a natural fermentation process. The result is a pungent and flavorful delicacy with a strong, distinctive aroma. Rakfisk is typically enjoyed during the winter months, and it is often served on flatbread accompanied by sour cream, finely chopped red onions, and a variety of herbs. The combination of the tangy fish, creamy sour cream, and the sharpness of the onions creates a complex and memorable taste experience. While the strong flavors of Rakfisk may be an acquired taste, it remains a beloved part of Norwegian culinary heritage.

Klippfisk:

Klippfisk, or dried and salted codfish, has played a vital role in Norwegian cuisine for centuries. This preservation method allowed the fish to be transported and stored for long periods, providing sustenance during times when fresh fish was not readily available. To prepare Klippfisk, the codfish is first dried in the open air, allowing it to become firm and leathery. Then it is heavily salted and left to cure for several weeks or months. When ready to be cooked, the fish is rehydrated by soaking it in water. Klippfisk is commonly used in the popular Norwegian dish called Bacalao. In this preparation, the rehydrated codfish is cooked with potatoes, onions, tomatoes, bell peppers, and garlic, often with a generous amount of olive oil. The result is a flavorful casserole that showcases the tender and flaky texture of the codfish, complemented by the robust flavors of the accompanying ingredients. Klippfisk has become an iconic ingredient in Norwegian cuisine, representing the history and ingenuity of the country's culinary traditions.

7.2. Seafood Delicacies:

Given its coastal location and proximity to the sea, seafood holds a special place in Norwegian cuisine, and Oslo is a city where seafood enthusiasts can indulge in a wide array of delicacies. Here are some must-try seafood dishes when exploring Oslo:

Gravlaks:

Gravlaks is a beloved Norwegian dish that showcases the delicate flavors of cured salmon. Thinly sliced, the salmon is traditionally cured with a mixture of salt, sugar, and dill, resulting in a tender and flavorful appetizer. The curing process imparts a subtle sweetness to the salmon while preserving its natural freshness. Gravlaks is often served with a traditional sweet mustard and dill sauce, which complements the richness of the fish. It is a popular choice for open-faced sandwiches, and the combination of flavors and textures creates a delightful culinary experience.

Prawns and Shrimp:

Norway is renowned for its high-quality prawns and shrimp. These crustaceans are a true delicacy and can be enjoyed in various forms. For a classic appetizer, shrimp cocktails are a popular choice, with succulent prawns served on a bed of fresh lettuce, accompanied by a tangy cocktail sauce. Prawn sandwiches are also a beloved option, featuring generous layers of shrimp on a buttered slice of bread, garnished with fresh lemon, mayonnaise, and perhaps a touch of dill. The simplicity of the dish allows the sweet and briny flavors of the prawns to shine.

Norwegian Lobster:

Norwegian lobster, known as "Hummer" in Norwegian, is a prized seafood delicacy. These lobsters are smaller than their American counterparts but pack an incredible flavor. Typically boiled to perfection, the Norwegian lobster is served with melted butter, a squeeze of lemon, and a side of freshly baked bread. The tender and sweet meat of the lobster, combined with the rich and creamy butter, creates a delectable combination that seafood enthusiasts will appreciate.

Scallops:

Oslo offers a variety of restaurants that excel in serving fresh and succulent scallops. Pan-seared to perfection, scallops are a delicate and elegant seafood option. The golden-brown sear on the outside reveals a tender and buttery interior. They are often served with a range of accompaniments that complement their flavors, such as crispy bacon, creamy pureed cauliflower, or a drizzle of nutty brown butter. The combination of flavors and textures creates a harmonious dish that highlights the natural sweetness of the scallops.

When exploring Oslo, seafood lovers will find themselves in a haven of delectable dishes. Whether it's the cured salmon of gravlaks, the succulent prawns and shrimp, the prized Norwegian lobster, or the delicate scallops, Oslo's seafood offerings are sure to satisfy even the most discerning palates.

7.3. Trendy Restaurants and Cafés:

Oslo is home to a vibrant and dynamic food scene, with numerous trendy restaurants and cafés catering to diverse tastes. Here are a few noteworthy establishments you should consider visiting:

Maaemo:

Maaemo stands as one of Oslo's most esteemed and prestigious restaurants, boasting an impressive three Michelin stars. With a strong focus on showcasing the best of Norwegian ingredients, Maaemo offers a culinary experience that is both innovative and artistically presented. The restaurant's menu reflects a deep appreciation for Norway's natural bounty, incorporating seasonal and locally sourced produce, foraged ingredients, and sustainable seafood. Each dish at Maaemo is a masterpiece, carefully crafted with meticulous attention to detail and an exploration of flavors, textures, and visual aesthetics. The chefs at Maaemo strive to push the boundaries of culinary creativity while maintaining a deep connection to Norwegian culinary traditions, resulting in a dining experience that is both extraordinary and unforgettable.

Smalhans:

Smalhans offers a refreshing departure from formal fine dining, embracing a relaxed and casual atmosphere while delivering exceptional cuisine. The restaurant's philosophy centers around simplicity and the use of high-quality ingredients. Smalhans showcases a ever-changing menu that features Nordic-inspired dishes with a modern twist, combining traditional flavors with contemporary techniques. The focus is on allowing the ingredients to shine, with each dish thoughtfully prepared to bring out their natural flavors and textures. Whether it's a comforting plate of perfectly cooked fish, a vibrant salad bursting with seasonal produce, or a delectable dessert crafted with finesse, Smalhans delivers a memorable dining experience that is both approachable and satisfying.

Tim Wendelboe:

For coffee enthusiasts, a visit to Tim Wendelboe is a must when exploring Oslo. This specialty coffee roastery and café is renowned for its dedication to sourcing and roasting their own beans, resulting in a unique and exceptional coffee experience. Tim Wendelboe's commitment to quality is evident in every cup they serve. The café offers a range of coffee options, from single-origin pour-overs to expertly crafted espresso-based beverages. The staff at Tim Wendelboe is passionate and knowledgeable, eager to share their expertise and guide visitors through the nuances of flavor profiles, brewing methods, and coffee origins. Whether you're a seasoned coffee connoisseur or simply appreciate a good cup of joe, Tim Wendelboe promises to deliver an unforgettable coffee experience that celebrates the art and science of coffee.

Mathallen Food Hall:

Nestled in the vibrant Vulkan area of Oslo, Mathallen Food Hall is a culinary haven that caters to every taste. The sprawling food hall houses a wide selection of food stalls, specialty shops, and restaurants, offering visitors a diverse range of cuisines and culinary experiences under one roof. From artisanal cheeses and cured meats to fresh seafood, organic produce, and international flavors, Mathallen showcases the best of local and global gastronomy. Whether you're in the mood for a quick bite, a leisurely meal, or simply browsing through the tantalizing displays of culinary delights, Mathallen offers a feast for the senses. It's the perfect place to indulge in gourmet treats, discover new flavors, and immerse yourself in the vibrant food culture of Oslo

7.4. Food Markets and Local Specialties:

For a taste of Oslo's local specialties and to immerse yourself in the city's culinary culture, exploring the food markets is a must. Here are a few notable food markets where you can discover local delights:

Oslo Farmers Market:

The Oslo Farmers Market is a bustling hub located in the heart of the city center, offering a vibrant and diverse array of local produce, artisanal products, and freshly baked goods. As you wander through the market, you'll be greeted by a kaleidoscope of colors and aromas, with stalls brimming with seasonal fruits, vegetables, and herbs. This is the perfect place to sample traditional Norwegian cheeses, which range from mild and creamy to pungent and aged, showcasing the rich diversity of Norwegian dairy craftsmanship. You'll also find a tempting selection of cured meats, such as the renowned fenalår (salted and cured lamb leg), along with homemade jams and preserves made from locally sourced berries. The market provides an authentic experience where you can connect with local producers, savor the flavors of the region, and bring home a taste of Oslo's culinary heritage.

Vulkan Fish Market:

Situated in close proximity to the Mathallen Food Hall, the Vulkan Fish Market is a haven for seafood enthusiasts. Here, you'll find a dazzling assortment of fresh fish, shellfish, and other seafood delicacies sourced directly from Norwegian waters. Immerse yourself in the briny aromas as you explore the stalls filled with glistening fish on ice, from succulent salmon and delicate trout to plump prawns and juicy scallops. The knowledgeable fishmongers are eager to share their expertise, helping you select the finest catches and offering advice on cooking techniques and flavor pairings.

Whether you're looking to create a lavish seafood feast or simply indulge in a quick and satisfying seafood snack, the Vulkan Fish Market is a treasure trove for discovering the finest flavors of the sea.

Grønland Market:

Located in Oslo's multicultural Grønland neighborhood, the Grønland Market is a bustling marketplace that offers a delightful fusion of international ingredients and spices. Here, you'll find a diverse range of culinary treasures from around the world, reflecting the multicultural fabric of Oslo. Take a stroll through the vibrant aisles, where aromatic spices from India, exotic fruits from Africa, and specialty ingredients from the Middle East beckon. Discover new flavors and pick up unique ingredients to infuse your culinary adventures with global influences. The market is not only a haven for home cooks seeking authentic flavors but also a gathering place for people from different backgrounds, fostering cultural exchange and appreciation through the universal language of food.

Bærums Verk:

A short distance from Oslo, Bærums Verk is a charming historic village that comes alive during the festive season with its traditional Norwegian Christmas market. Step into a winter wonderland as you meander through the market stalls adorned with twinkling lights and festive decorations. Indulge in traditional Norwegian treats that evoke a sense of nostalgia and warmth, such as lefse, a delicate potato flatbread often served with butter and sugar, or krumkake, delicate waffle cookies that are rolled and filled with cream.

Sip on gløgg, a spiced and mulled wine infused with flavors of cinnamon, cloves, and orange peel, which will envelop you in the cozy ambiance of the season. The market offers a charming glimpse into Norway's rich Christmas traditions, allowing you to experience the joy and flavors of the festive season in a picturesque setting.

Exploring these markets and trying local specialties will give you a genuine taste of Oslo's culinary heritage and the opportunity to engage with the local food culture.

CHAPTER EIGHT

Shopping in Oslo

8.1. Karl Johans Gate:

Karl Johans Gate, named after King Charles III John, is not just a shopping street but a cultural and historical hub in Oslo. Stretching from the Royal Palace to Oslo Central Station, it offers a captivating blend of retail therapy, architectural wonders, and lively entertainment.

As you embark on your stroll down Karl Johans Gate, you'll be greeted by a wide range of shops and boutiques catering to diverse tastes. International fashion brands like H&M, Zara, and Mango showcase the latest trends, while local designers exhibit their unique creations, infusing Scandinavian aesthetics into their designs. It's a fashion lover's paradise, where you can find everything from high-street fashion to high-end luxury.

For those seeking a taste of Norwegian culture, Karl Johans Gate also houses traditional specialty stores. Step into charming shops offering handcrafted items, such as intricate woodwork, exquisite silverware, and traditional Norwegian clothing known as bunads. These stores provide an authentic experience, allowing you to take home a piece of Norwegian craftsmanship and heritage.

Beyond shopping, Karl Johans Gate is steeped in history and architecture. As you wander along the street, you'll encounter architectural gems that have stood the test of time. The Parliament Building (Stortinget), with its grand neoclassical façade, stands as a symbol of Norwegian democracy. The University of Oslo, with its stunning buildings and beautiful surroundings, exudes an academic ambiance that adds to the street's charm.

The lively atmosphere of Karl Johans Gate is enhanced by the frequent street performances, art displays, and events that take place here. Talented musicians, artists, and performers often grace the street, infusing it with their creative energy. It's not uncommon to stumble upon live music, captivating street art, or cultural festivities while exploring this vibrant thoroughfare.

Karl Johans Gate is not just a shopping destination; it's an immersive experience that encapsulates the essence of Oslo's dynamic spirit. Whether you're indulging in retail therapy, marveling at architectural wonders, or soaking in the cultural atmosphere, this iconic street is sure to leave a lasting impression on your visit to Oslo.

8.2. Bogstadveien Shopping Street:

Situated in the affluent Majorstuen neighborhood, Bogstadveien stands out as one of Oslo's premier shopping streets. Renowned for its trendy and fashionable offerings, this vibrant street caters to fashionistas and style-conscious individuals seeking the latest trends and high-quality products.

As you wander along Bogstadveien, you'll be captivated by the wide array of clothing stores, shoe shops, accessories boutiques, and interior design outlets that line the street. From international luxury brands to renowned Scandinavian designers, the options are diverse and enticing. Discover elegant fashion pieces, stylish footwear, and accessories that reflect the cutting-edge aesthetics of contemporary fashion.

Bogstadveien is not solely dedicated to fashion; it also entices culinary enthusiasts. The street is home to an enticing variety of cafes, bakeries, and restaurants where you can take a break from shopping and treat yourself to delectable delights. Enjoy freshly brewed coffee, indulge in mouthwatering pastries, or savor a delicious meal prepared with local ingredients. Bogstadveien offers a perfect blend of shopping and gastronomic pleasures.

Beyond its shopping and culinary offerings, Bogstadveien's charm extends to its surrounding neighborhood. Take a moment to explore the streets that branch off from the main thoroughfare and soak up the local ambiance. Discover hidden boutiques, charming parks, and quaint streets dotted with unique shops and cafes. The atmosphere is lively, bustling, and infused with a sense of urban charm that adds to the overall appeal of Bogstadveien.

Whether you're seeking a refined shopping experience, culinary delights, or a chance to immerse yourself in the local ambiance, Bogstadveien offers it all. With its blend of upscale shopping options, trendy eateries, and a vibrant neighborhood, this iconic street beckons to those who appreciate the finer things in life

8.3. Grünerløkka's Boutique Stores:

Grünerløkka, a vibrant and trendy neighborhood in Oslo, is renowned for its creative and alternative scene. It serves as a haven for artists, designers, and independent businesses, making it a captivating destination for discovering unique boutique stores and immersing oneself in a vibrant artistic atmosphere.

The streets of Grünerløkka are a treasure trove of eclectic fashion boutiques, concept stores, vintage shops, and art galleries. Here, you'll encounter a fusion of contemporary Scandinavian designs, retro fashion finds, and locally crafted accessories. The neighborhood's artistic spirit is reflected in the diverse range of shops, allowing you to explore narrow streets and hidden corners, uncovering hidden gems and one-of-a-kind items that embody Grünerløkka's creative essence.

Fashion is just one facet of Grünerløkka's allure. The neighborhood also boasts specialty stores catering to niche interests, such as vinyl records, handmade crafts, organic beauty products, and more. This emphasis on individuality and creativity creates a refreshing and diverse shopping experience, where you can find unique items that align with your personal style and passions.

Beyond the shopping experience, Grünerløkka offers a vibrant social scene that complements its artistic vibe. Explore trendy cafes, bustling markets, and cozy bars, where you can mingle with locals, fellow art enthusiasts, and creative minds. The neighborhood's lively atmosphere invites you to immerse yourself in its dynamic energy, whether you're savoring a cup of coffee, browsing through artisanal goods, or simply enjoying the ambiance.

Grünerløkka's boutique stores are a testament to Oslo's thriving creative community. They showcase the city's commitment to nurturing artistic expression and provide a platform for local designers and artisans to share their craft with the world. Exploring these stores offers a unique opportunity to connect with Oslo's creative pulse and discover treasures that embody the neighborhood's vibrant spirit.

Whether you're seeking fashionable finds, unique artwork, or a chance to experience a bustling creative hub, Grünerløkka offers an inviting blend of art, culture, and individuality. Embrace the neighborhood's artistic energy, immerse yourself in its vibrant social scene, and let Grünerløkka's boutique stores guide you on a journey of artistic exploration and self-expression.

8.4. Souvenirs and Norwegian Design:

No visit to Oslo is complete without immersing yourself in the world of Norwegian design and culture. The city offers a treasure trove of options for souvenir shopping, allowing you to bring home a piece of Norway's rich artistic heritage.

Start your journey by exploring specialty stores and markets that showcase the impeccable craftsmanship and design that Norway is renowned for. These establishments exhibit a wide range of traditional handicrafts, each with its own story to tell. Admire intricately carved wooden figures, meticulously knitted woolen sweaters adorned with traditional patterns, and exquisite silver jewelry inspired by Viking heritage. These timeless treasures not only make for cherished mementos but also serve as meaningful gifts for your loved ones, carrying a piece of Norwegian culture with them.

If you're drawn to contemporary design, Oslo has a vibrant scene that caters to your taste. Venture into shops that highlight the country's modern aesthetics and discover a world of sleek and stylish home decor items, innovative furniture pieces, and fashion accessories crafted by local designers. Scandinavian minimalism, functional design, and sustainable materials often define these unique pieces, embodying the essence of Norwegian modernity.

To delve deeper into the evolution of Norwegian design, consider visiting design museums and galleries scattered throughout Oslo. These institutions provide a deeper understanding of the artistic movements, influences, and innovations that have shaped Norwegian design over the years. Gain insights into the cultural significance of design in Norway and its impact on the global design scene. It's an opportunity to appreciate the creativity and ingenuity that defines Oslo's design heritage.

Regardless of whether you choose traditional souvenirs or contemporary design pieces, Oslo offers a wide range of options to suit every taste. Embrace the beauty of Norwegian craftsmanship and bring a piece of Oslo's design heritage back home with you. Each item serves as a tangible reminder of your journey and allows you to share a part of Oslo's artistic soul with others. So, indulge in the artistry, immerse yourself in the world of Norwegian design, and treasure the memories that these souvenirs hold.

CHAPTER NINE

Nightlife and Entertainment

9.1. Bars and Pubs

When it comes to bars and pubs, Oslo offers a vibrant and diverse scene to cater to every taste. Whether you're looking for a cozy neighborhood pub or a trendy cocktail bar, you'll find plenty of options to enjoy a night out in the city. Here are some notable bars and pubs in Oslo:

a) Himkok: Himkok is not just a bar but an experience for cocktail enthusiasts in Oslo. Renowned for its innovative craft cocktails, this establishment takes pride in using locally sourced ingredients to create unique and flavorful drinks. The talented mixologists at Himkok are known for their creativity and attention to detail, crafting exquisite concoctions that push the boundaries of mixology. The bar's stylish ambiance adds to the overall experience, with its sleek and modern design creating a sophisticated atmosphere for guests to enjoy their handcrafted drinks. From classic cocktails with a twist to signature creations, Himkok is a must-visit destination for those seeking a memorable and delightful drinking experience in Oslo.

b) Torggata Botaniske: Tucked away in the heart of Oslo, Torggata Botaniske is a hidden gem for cocktail enthusiasts. This botanical-themed bar offers a vast selection of botanical-infused cocktails, making it a haven for those who appreciate the art of mixology. The atmosphere is relaxed and welcoming, providing an ideal spot to unwind and enjoy a drink with friends. The bartenders at Torggata Botaniske are skilled in their craft, using a variety of herbs, fruits, and botanicals to create refreshing and aromatic cocktails that tantalize the taste buds. Whether you prefer a classic gin and tonic with a botanical twist or an inventive floral concoction, Torggata Botaniske promises an immersive and flavorful experience in the heart of Oslo.

c) Schouskjelleren Mikrobryggeri: For beer enthusiasts, Schouskjelleren Mikrobryggeri is a must-visit destination in Oslo. Located in the former Schous Brewery, this microbrewery embodies the rich brewing culture of the city. With a wide range of craft beers on tap, including their own brews, Schouskjelleren offers a true taste of Oslo's vibrant beer scene. From hoppy IPAs to rich stouts and refreshing lagers, beer lovers will find a diverse selection to satisfy their palates. The knowledgeable staff at Schouskjelleren are passionate about their craft and are happy to provide recommendations and insights into the brewing process. The brewery's cozy and welcoming atmosphere creates an inviting space where visitors can relax, socialize, and enjoy the art of brewing in the heart of Oslo.

d) Fuglen: Fuglen is not your typical bar—it's a unique concept that combines a coffee shop, bar, and vintage design boutique into one trendy establishment. With a retro vibe and impeccable attention to detail, Fuglen has become a popular destination for those seeking a stylish and memorable drinking experience. The bar offers a range of carefully crafted cocktails and spirits, each prepared with precision and expertise by their expert mixologists. Whether you're in the mood for a classic cocktail or an inventive creation, Fuglen's menu is sure to impress. The vintage design boutique adds to the ambiance, allowing visitors to explore and appreciate the curated selection of retro furniture and decor. Fuglen promises an unforgettable drinking experience that seamlessly blends the worlds of coffee, cocktails, and design into a unique and vibrant atmosphere..

9.2. Live Music Venues

For music lovers, Oslo boasts a thriving live music scene with venues catering to various genres and tastes. Whether you're into rock, jazz, indie, or electronic music, there are venues that host talented local and international artists. Here are some notable live music venues in Oslo:

a) Rockefeller Music Hall: Rockefeller Music Hall is a legendary venue in Oslo that has become synonymous with unforgettable live music experiences. It has a reputation for hosting concerts by both established and emerging artists across various genres. The venue boasts an excellent sound system that ensures pristine audio quality, allowing concert-goers to fully immerse themselves in the music. With its spacious dance floor and comfortable seating areas, Rockefeller Music Hall provides ample space for fans to enjoy their favorite artists' performances. Whether you're into rock, pop, electronic, or alternative music, Rockefeller Music Hall offers an unparalleled concert experience that leaves a lasting impression.

b) Blå: Nestled along the picturesque banks of the Akerselva River, Blå stands out as a vibrant and eclectic live music venue in Oslo. This multi-level establishment has gained a reputation for its diverse lineup of live bands and DJs, showcasing a wide range of musical genres. From jazz and world music to electronic beats and experimental sounds, Blå caters to music enthusiasts of all tastes. The venue's intimate and welcoming atmosphere, adorned with colorful artwork and graffiti, creates a unique ambiance that complements the diverse performances on stage. Whether you're discovering emerging artists or enjoying the sounds of established musicians, Blå promises an exciting and dynamic music experience against the backdrop of Oslo's beautiful riverside.

c) Oslo Jazzhus: As the name suggests, Oslo Jazzhus is a haven for jazz lovers in the city. This intimate and cozy venue is dedicated to promoting jazz music and hosts an array of local and international jazz musicians. With its warm and inviting atmosphere, Oslo Jazzhus creates an intimate setting that allows the audience to truly immerse themselves in the captivating sounds of jazz. From smooth improvisations to energetic ensembles, the venue showcases the depth and versatility of the genre. Whether you're a seasoned jazz aficionado or simply curious about exploring the world of jazz, Oslo Jazzhus offers an intimate and immersive jazz experience that will transport you into the captivating realm of this timeless genre.

d) Revolver: Located in the heart of Oslo's music scene, Revolver is a dynamic and energetic venue that has become a favorite among alternative and indie music enthusiasts. The venue hosts live concerts, club nights, and DJ sets, catering to a diverse range of musical tastes. With its gritty and underground atmosphere, Revolver creates an authentic and unapologetic space for music enthusiasts to come together and celebrate alternative sounds. The energetic vibes and pulsating beats that fill the venue make it an ideal destination for those seeking an electrifying live music experience. Whether you're discovering emerging artists or reveling in the sounds of your favorite indie bands, Revolver guarantees an unforgettable night of music, dancing, and camaraderie.

9.3. Nightclubs and DJ Sets

a) Jæger: Jæger is a mecca for electronic music lovers in Oslo. Situated in the heart of the city, this underground club is renowned for its cutting-edge techno, house, and disco music. Jæger showcases both local and international DJs who are at the forefront of the electronic music scene. The club's immersive atmosphere, with its dim lighting and pulsating beats, sets the stage for an unforgettable night of non-stop dancing. With its dedication to promoting underground sounds and its passionate crowd of music enthusiasts, Jæger is a must-visit destination for those seeking a truly immersive and electrifying nightclub experience in Oslo.

b) The Villa: Housed in a beautifully renovated townhouse, The Villa stands out as one of Oslo's most sophisticated and upscale nightclubs. The venue boasts a state-of-the-art sound system that ensures impeccable audio quality and an immersive experience for clubbers. The music programming at The Villa is diverse, catering to a wide range of tastes including electronic beats, house, and hip-hop. Renowned DJs grace the decks, delivering memorable sets that keep the dance floor moving all night long. The elegant interior design, with its atmospheric lighting and stylish decor, creates a refined ambiance that complements the high-quality music programming. Whether you're seeking an evening of grooving to electronic beats or a night of hip-hop-infused energy, The Villa promises a memorable and upscale nightclub experience in Oslo.

c) BLÅ: Known primarily as a live music venue, BLÅ seamlessly transitions into a vibrant nightclub after hours. The club features multiple dance floors, each with its own distinct vibe and music selection. From electronic and house to alternative and indie tracks, BLÅ offers a diverse range of genres that cater to different tastes. The energetic atmosphere, combined with the club's riverside location, creates a unique and captivating setting for a night of dancing and revelry. Whether you're a fan of electronic beats or prefer the raw energy of live bands, BLÅ provides a one-of-a-kind nightclub experience that showcases Oslo's vibrant and eclectic nightlife scene.

d) Dattera til Hagen: Dattera til Hagen is a multi-level venue that seamlessly combines a café, bar, and nightclub into one vibrant space. Throughout the day, it serves as a bustling café and bar, attracting locals and visitors alike. As the night falls, Dattera til Hagen transforms into a lively nightclub with an infectious energy. The venue hosts various DJ sets, spanning a wide range of genres including electronic music, hip-hop, and more. The eclectic music selection ensures that there is something for everyone, enticing partygoers to hit the dance floor and let loose. With its multi-level layout, stylish interior, and lively atmosphere, Dattera til Hagen guarantees a night of fun, music, and unforgettable memories in the heart of Oslo's nightlife.

9.4. Performing Arts in Oslo

For those seeking a dose of culture and the performing arts, Oslo offers a range of venues and events showcasing theater, ballet, opera, and more. Here are some highlights of Oslo's performing arts scene:

a) Jæger: Jæger is a mecca for electronic music lovers in Oslo. Situated in the heart of the city, this underground club is renowned for its cutting-edge techno, house, and disco music. Jæger showcases both local and international DJs who are at the forefront of the electronic music scene. The club's immersive atmosphere, with its dim lighting and pulsating beats, sets the stage for an unforgettable night of non-stop dancing. With its dedication to promoting underground sounds and its passionate crowd of music enthusiasts, Jæger is a must-visit destination for those seeking a truly immersive and electrifying nightclub experience in Oslo.

b) The Villa: Housed in a beautifully renovated townhouse, The Villa stands out as one of Oslo's most sophisticated and upscale nightclubs. The venue boasts a state-of-the-art sound system that ensures impeccable audio quality and an immersive experience for clubbers. The music programming at The Villa is diverse, catering to a wide range of tastes including electronic beats, house, and hip-hop. Renowned DJs grace the decks, delivering memorable sets that keep the dance floor moving all night long. The elegant interior design, with its atmospheric lighting and stylish decor, creates a refined ambiance that complements the high-quality music programming. Whether you're seeking an evening of grooving to electronic beats or a night of hip-hop-infused energy, The Villa promises a memorable and upscale nightclub experience in Oslo.

c) BLÅ: Known primarily as a live music venue, BLÅ seamlessly transitions into a vibrant nightclub after hours. The club features multiple dance floors, each with its own distinct vibe and music selection. From electronic and house to alternative and indie tracks, BLÅ offers a diverse range of genres that cater to different tastes. The energetic atmosphere, combined with the club's riverside location, creates a unique and captivating setting for a night of dancing and revelry. Whether you're a fan of electronic beats or prefer the raw energy of live bands, BLÅ provides a one-of-a-kind nightclub experience that showcases Oslo's vibrant and eclectic nightlife scene.

d) Dattera til Hagen: Dattera til Hagen is a multi-level venue that seamlessly combines a café, bar, and nightclub into one vibrant space. Throughout the day, it serves as a bustling café and bar, attracting locals and visitors alike. As the night falls, Dattera til Hagen transforms into a lively nightclub with an infectious energy. The venue hosts various DJ sets, spanning a wide range of genres including electronic music, hip-hop, and more. The eclectic music selection ensures that there is something for everyone, enticing partygoers to hit the dance floor and let loose. With its multi-level layout, stylish interior, and lively atmosphere, Dattera til Hagen guarantees a night of fun, music, and unforgettable memories in the heart of Oslo's nighta) Oslo Opera House: The Oslo Opera House is an architectural marvel that has become an iconic symbol of the city. Its sleek and modern design, resembling a glacier rising from the Oslofjord, captures the attention of both locals and visitors alike. Beyond its stunning exterior, the Opera House is a cultural powerhouse, hosting world-class opera, ballet, and classical music performances. Inside the venue, the acoustics are finely tuned to create an immersive experience for the audience, allowing them to be swept away by the emotive power of the performances. From captivating operas to graceful ballet performances and orchestral concerts, the Oslo Opera House offers a range of artistic experiences that will leave a lasting impression on art enthusiasts and cultural explorers.

b) Nationaltheatret: Nationaltheatret holds a special place in the heart of Norwegian theater enthusiasts. This historic theater showcases an impressive repertoire of plays, ranging from classic Norwegian dramas to thought-provoking international works. As one of Norway's premier theaters, Nationaltheatret attracts top-tier actors, directors, and playwrights, ensuring that every production is of the highest quality. Stepping into the theater, visitors are greeted by an elegant and atmospheric space that exudes a sense of theatrical grandeur. From intense dramas to lighthearted comedies and thought-provoking contemporary pieces, Nationaltheatret offers a diverse range of theatrical experiences that showcase the richness of Norwegian and international theater.

c) Chat Noir: Established in 1912, Chat Noir holds the distinction of being Norway's oldest revue theater. Throughout its long and storied history, it has delighted audiences with its entertaining and comedic shows. Combining elements of music, dance, and satire, Chat Noir presents revue performances that are filled with laughter, wit, and memorable moments. The theater's intimate setting creates an immersive experience, allowing the audience to feel connected to the performers and fully engage with the humor and entertainment on stage. With its lively atmosphere, talented cast, and a rich tradition of comedic excellence, a visit to Chat Noir promises an unforgettable evening of entertainment that will have you laughing, tapping your feet, and humming along to catchy tunes.

d) Folketeateret: Folketeateret is a grand theater that has become synonymous with spectacular musical productions in Oslo. The venue has a long-standing tradition of hosting large-scale musicals, featuring both international hits and Norwegian adaptations. From beloved Broadway classics to contemporary favorites, Folketeateret presents theatrical experiences that are visually stunning, emotionally engaging, and musically enchanting. The theater's spacious auditorium, adorned with opulent decor and state-of-the-art technology, creates a captivating setting for audiences to immerse themselves in the magic of live theater. With its top-notch performances, lavish sets, and extraordinary talent, Folketeateret offers an unforgettable theatrical experience that celebrates the art of storytelling through song, dance, and mesmerizing performances .life.

Whether you're interested in music, nightlife, or the performing arts, Oslo's vibrant and diverse scene is sure to captivate and entertain visitors from all walks of life.

CHAPTER TEN

Day Trips from Oslo

10.1. The Norwegian Countryside

Exploring the Norwegian Countryside: Immerse yourself in the breathtaking natural beauty that surrounds Oslo. From rolling hills covered in lush green landscapes to charming villages nestled amidst serene lakes, the Norwegian countryside offers a captivating escape from the bustling city life.

Hiking Trails and Nature Walks: Lace up your hiking boots and embark on a journey through a network of scenic trails and nature walks. Wind your way through untouched forests, where rays of sunlight filter through the canopy, creating a magical atmosphere. As you traverse the trails, keep an eye out for wildlife that calls this pristine environment home. You may spot deer gracefully leaping through the undergrowth or catch a glimpse of a red squirrel darting between the trees. Reaching the mountaintops rewards you with awe-inspiring panoramic views of the surrounding landscapes, where fjords and valleys stretch out as far as the eye can see.

Charming Farmsteads and Rural Life: Step into the heart of traditional Norwegian rural life by visiting charming farmsteads dotted throughout the countryside. Engage with friendly locals who are passionate about their land and way of life. Learn about their sustainable farming practices, passed down through generations, which prioritize harmony with nature and the preservation of the environment. Experience the joy of picking your own fruits and vegetables straight from the fields, or indulge in the taste of freshly baked bread made from locally sourced grains. Immerse yourself in the tranquil ambiance of the countryside, where time seems to slow down, allowing you to appreciate the simple pleasures of life.

Fishing and River Activities: For fishing enthusiasts, the Norwegian countryside offers a paradise of angling opportunities. Cast your line into crystal-clear rivers and tranquil lakes, teeming with an abundance of fish species. Feel the anticipation and excitement as you wait for a tug on the line, signaling a possible encounter with a wild salmon or a spirited trout. Whether you prefer fly fishing in a babbling brook or setting sail on a peaceful lake, the pristine waters of the Norwegian countryside offer an unforgettable experience for both seasoned anglers and beginners alike.

Wildlife Encounters: Embark on a wildlife adventure in the Norwegian countryside, where nature's wonders unfold before your eyes. Explore carefully protected nature reserves and national parks dedicated to preserving Norway's diverse wildlife. As you venture into these pristine habitats, you may come across majestic reindeer, their impressive antlers crowning their heads, or encounter the elusive moose, gracefully navigating through the underbrush. Keep your binoculars handy to observe a variety of bird species in their natural habitats, from the magnificent golden eagle soaring through the sky to the colorful puffins nesting along the rugged coastal cliffs. These encounters with Norway's captivating wildlife provide an opportunity to deepen your appreciation for the delicate balance of nature and the importance of its preservation.

In the Norwegian countryside surrounding Oslo, nature's beauty unfolds in every direction. Whether you're exploring the enchanting hiking trails, embracing the tranquility of rural life, angling in pristine waters, or observing the wonders of wildlife, the countryside offers a chance to connect with nature, rejuvenate the soul, and create lifelong memories of Norway's natural wonders

10.2. The Oslofjord Islands

Island-Hopping in the Oslofjord: Unveiling the Gems of Norway's Coastal Wonderland

Introduction:

The Oslofjord, a magnificent natural marvel, beckons travelers to escape the bustling city and embark on an unforgettable island-hopping journey. Each island in this collection holds its own unique allure, with a tapestry of history, breathtaking landscapes, and captivating attractions waiting to be discovered. From the historic ruins of Hovedøya Island to the tranquil oasis of Gressholmen Island, and the recreational haven of Langøyene Island, this expedition promises an immersive experience filled with beauty, serenity, and a deeper understanding of Norway's coastal heritage.

Hovedøya Island: A Journey into History, Nature, and Blissful Seclusion

As your adventure commences, Hovedøya Island unfolds before you, enticing with its rich history and unspoiled beauty. Step ashore and immerse yourself in the ancient monastery ruins, remnants of a bygone era that whisper tales of spiritual devotion and architectural grandeur. Stroll along the sandy beaches, feel the cool breeze gently caressing your face, and bask in the warm embrace of the sun as you indulge in a leisurely picnic amidst the lush greenery. For those seeking a refreshing respite, take a dip in the crystal-clear waters of the fjord, revitalizing your senses and connecting with the tranquil spirit of nature. Hovedøya Island also offers scenic walking trails, guiding you through verdant landscapes, where fragrant wildflowers sway in harmony with the wind and panoramic vistas of the fjord unfold at every turn.

Gressholmen Island: A Gateway to Serenity, Nature, and Reflection

Continuing your island-hopping odyssey, Gressholmen Island invites you into its tranquil embrace, where lush forests and idyllic landscapes create an oasis of serenity. As you step foot onto the island, a sense of calm envelops you, as if time itself has slowed down. Embark on a leisurely walk along the meandering paths, enveloped by the rustling leaves and the melodic songs of birds. The verdant greenery offers a sanctuary for contemplation and introspection, allowing you to connect with the innate harmony of the natural world. Find a secluded spot to spread out a picnic blanket and savor the simple pleasures of life, surrounded by panoramic fjord views that seem to stretch to eternity. Gressholmen Island, with its serene ambiance and untouched beauty, is a sanctuary for weary souls in search of tranquility and a deeper connection with nature.

Langøyene Island: A Haven of Recreation, Adventure, and Beachside Bliss

Your island-hopping escapade would not be complete without a visit to Langøyene Island, a sought-after recreational destination that caters to all desires. Set foot on its sandy beaches, where the golden grains caress your toes, and the rhythmic waves serenade you with their soothing melody. Unwind by the water's edge, gazing out at the horizon as the sun paints the sky with hues of gold and orange, creating a spectacle that ignites the soul. Engage in invigorating water sports, from kayaking to paddleboarding, immersing yourself in the thrill of the fjord's embrace. The island's hiking trails beckon adventurers to explore, offering scenic routes that wind through diverse landscapes, where hidden treasures await to be uncovered. Find respite in the designated BBQ areas, where the aroma of grilled delicacies mingles with laughter and conversation, forging unforgettable memories against the backdrop of stunning fjord views.

Historical Gems: Unearthing Norway's Coastal Defense and Maritime Legacy

As you traverse the Oslofjord, the islands reveal historical gems that bear witness to Norway's maritime heritage and coastal defense. Encounter the remnants of old fortifications, which stand as testament to the strategic importance of the region throughout history. These silent sentinels, once guarding against potential invasions, now offer glimpses into the past, enabling you to envision the valor and sacrifice that shaped Norway's coastal defense. Explore the lighthouses that proudly stand along the fjord's edge, their beacons guiding ships through treacherous waters and serving as symbols of hope and safety. Each lighthouse carries tales of daring rescues, steadfast resilience, and the maritime spirit that courses through Norway's veins. Delve into cultural landmarks that dot the islands, unveiling the rich tapestry of Norway's traditions, artistry, and storytelling. Museums, art installations, and historical buildings provide insight into the vibrant cultural fabric that weaves together the coastal communities.

Conclusion:

Island-hopping through the Oslofjord is a transcendent journey that intertwines nature's splendor, historical narratives, and the serenity of the fjord's embrace. From the ancient monastery ruins of Hovedøya Island to the secluded bliss of Gressholmen Island, and the recreational haven of Langøyene Island, each destination captivates the senses and beckons the explorer within. As you uncover the historical gems scattered across the islands, you develop a profound appreciation for Norway's coastal defense and maritime legacy. The Oslofjord's islands offer respite from the demands of modern life, inviting you to immerse yourself in the beauty, serenity, and cultural tapestry that make this corner of the world truly extraordinary. So, set sail, embrace the allure of the Oslofjord, and embark on an island-hopping adventure that will leave an indelible mark on your heart and soul.

10.3. Historical Towns and Landmarks

Historical Treasures: Unraveling Norway's Captivating Past

Introduction:

Embarking on a journey beyond the city limits of Oslo, you'll discover a tapestry of historical towns and landmarks that offer a captivating glimpse into Norway's rich heritage. From well-preserved medieval towns to ancient ruins and architectural marvels, each destination paints a vivid picture of the country's intriguing past. Prepare to be transported through time as you explore these enchanting locations, immersing yourself in their stories and marveling at their architectural splendor.

Drammen: Where History Meets Modernity

Your first stop on this historical expedition is the charming city of Drammen, known for its well-preserved 18th-century architecture and scenic riverside promenades. As you wander through its cobblestone streets, you'll be captivated by the architectural gems that line the way. Admire the elegant facades of the historic buildings, showcasing a blend of traditional Norwegian design and European influences. The city's vibrant cultural scene is also worth exploring, with art galleries, theaters, and museums offering a window into Drammen's creative spirit. Take a leisurely stroll along the riverside promenades, where the tranquil waters of the Drammen River reflect the city's colorful facades, creating a picturesque backdrop that perfectly encapsulates the fusion of history and modernity.

Fredrikstad: Stepping into the Past

Prepare to step back in time as you arrive in Fredrikstad, one of Northern Europe's best-preserved fortified towns. The sight of its medieval walls rising proudly from the ground is a testament to the town's rich history and cultural heritage. Explore the cobbled streets, which wind their way through the heart of the town, leading you to charming squares, hidden courtyards, and historic landmarks. Marvel at the intricate details of the preserved architecture, from timber-framed houses to imposing gates. As you walk along the ramparts, a sense of awe washes over you, allowing you to imagine the lives of those who once defended the town from invaders. Immerse yourself in Fredrikstad's vibrant history by visiting museums, such as the Fredrikstad Museum, where artifacts and exhibitions provide further insight into the town's fascinating past.

Tønsberg: Norway's Ancient Heritage

Journeying further into the annals of Norwegian history, you'll arrive in Tønsberg, the country's oldest town, where echoes of the past resonate through its streets. Explore the impressive ruins of Tønsberg Castle, a medieval fortress that once stood as a symbol of power and authority. Walk in the footsteps of ancient Vikings as you visit the local museum, delving into Tønsberg's rich Viking heritage and uncovering artifacts that bring their stories to life. Tønsberg's vibrant harbor area offers a picturesque setting to relax and observe the interplay between history and modern life. Listen to the lapping waves and inhale the salty sea breeze as you soak in the ambiance of a town that has witnessed centuries of change.

Hamar: Where History Unfolds

Nestled by the serene waters of Lake Mjøsa, Hamar invites you to delve into its captivating history. The crown jewel of the town is the magnificent Hamar Cathedral, a medieval masterpiece that showcases the architectural prowess of the era. Marvel at the soaring arches, intricate stained glass windows, and ornate decorations that adorn this sacred space. Step outside and explore the open-air museum of Domkirkeodden, an archaeological site that reveals the town's Viking past. Wander through the remains of Hamar's first cathedral, explore reconstructed Viking longhouses, and gain insight into the daily lives of these ancient seafarers. As you stroll along the lakefront, breathtaking views unfold before you, providing a serene backdrop to reflect upon the layers of history that have shaped Hamar.

Conclusion:

As you conclude your exploration of these historical towns and landmarks surrounding Oslo, you'll carry with you a deeper understanding of Norway's captivating past. From the well-preserved architecture of Drammen to the fortified walls of Fredrikstad, the ancient ruins of Tønsberg, and the medieval grandeur of Hamar Cathedral, each destination has left an indelible mark on your journey. These historical treasures not only serve as windows into the past but also highlight the enduring spirit of the Norwegian people and their connection to their heritage. So, continue your voyage through time, immersing yourself in the captivating narratives woven into the fabric of these remarkable destinations.

10.4. Outdoor Adventures Near Oslo

Nature Reserves and National Parks: Embracing the Majesty of Oslo's Outdoors

Introduction:

Beyond the vibrant cityscape of Oslo lies a natural paradise awaiting exploration. Venture into the surrounding areas and discover a wealth of outdoor adventures in nature reserves and national parks. From dense forests and sparkling lakes to rugged mountains, these diverse landscapes offer a playground for outdoor enthusiasts. Whether you seek serenity in the tranquility of a forest or adrenaline-pumping activities amidst majestic peaks, Oslo's surrounding nature reserves and national parks have something to offer everyone.

Nordmarka Forest: A Wilderness on Oslo's Doorstep

Embark on a thrilling escapade into Nordmarka Forest, a vast wilderness located just outside Oslo. Lace up your hiking boots or hop on your bicycle and venture into this natural playground. Follow the marked trails that crisscross through the forest, leading you deeper into its heart. As you make your way, listen to the harmonious symphony of birdsong and the rustle of leaves underfoot. Spot wildlife in their natural habitat, from elusive deer to curious foxes. Take a moment to breathe in the crisp, clean air and bask in the peacefulness that surrounds you. Nordmarka Forest offers a sanctuary for those seeking respite from the urban bustle, inviting you to connect with nature and revel in its wonders.

Bygdøy Peninsula: Where Nature Meets Coastal Beauty

Experience the best of Oslo's outdoor offerings on the picturesque Bygdøy Peninsula. This idyllic coastal haven beckons with its sandy beaches, lush green spaces, and breathtaking views. Take a leisurely coastal walk, allowing the soothing sound of crashing waves to accompany your footsteps. As you stroll along, soak in the panoramic vistas of the sparkling Oslofjord, dotted with sailboats and shimmering in the sunlight. For a more adventurous experience, rent a kayak and glide across the tranquil waters, exploring hidden coves and secluded beaches. Alternatively, hop on a bicycle and pedal your way along the coastline, feeling the gentle sea breeze caress your face. Bygdøy Peninsula is a true oasis where nature seamlessly merges with coastal beauty, offering a tranquil escape from the hustle and bustle of city life.

Embracing Winter: A Playground for Snow Enthusiasts

When winter blankets the landscape around Oslo, a whole new realm of outdoor activities emerges. Embrace the winter wonderland and engage in an array of exciting winter sports. Oslomarka, the vast forested area surrounding the city, transforms into a snowy paradise for cross-country skiing and snowshoeing enthusiasts. Strap on your skis and glide along the meticulously groomed trails, marveling at the serene beauty of snow-clad trees and frozen lakes. Alternatively, don a pair of snowshoes and venture off the beaten path, immersing yourself in the pristine wilderness. For an unforgettable experience, try dog sledding, where a team of energetic huskies pulls you through the snowy landscapes, creating memories that will last a lifetime. If you crave the thrill of downhill skiing or snowboarding, nearby ski resorts offer well-groomed slopes catering to all skill levels. Immerse yourself in the exhilarating winter sports scene, where adrenaline and snowflakes intertwine.

Hiking and Climbing: Reaching New Heights

For those who yearn for the thrill of reaching new heights, the surrounding mountains and hills near Oslo offer an abundance of opportunities for hiking and climbing. Strap on your backpack and embark on a challenging hike that rewards you with stunning viewpoints and panoramic vistas. Ascend to peaks that offer breathtaking views of Oslo, the surrounding fjords, and the distant horizon. Traverse through rugged terrain, feeling the exhilaration of conquering nature's obstacles. For the more experienced climbers, there are cliffs and rock faces waiting to be conquered. Test your skills and feel the rush of adrenaline as you scale the vertical surfaces, relying on your strength, technique, and the support of fellow climbers. Oslo's surrounding landscapes provide the perfect backdrop for outdoor adventurers seeking to push their limits and be rewarded with unforgettable vistas.

Conclusion:

As you delve into the nature reserves and national parks surrounding Oslo, you'll find yourself immersed in the majesty of the Norwegian outdoors. Nordmarka Forest's sprawling wilderness, the coastal beauty of Bygdøy Peninsula, the winter wonderland of Oslomarka, and the thrill of hiking and climbing in the mountains all offer unique experiences that connect you with nature and ignite your sense of adventure. So, venture beyond the city's limits and embrace the wonders of Oslo's surrounding landscapes, where nature invites you to explore, rejuvenate, and create memories that will last a lifetime.

CHAPTER ELEVEN

Practical Information and Tips

11.1. Safety and Security:

Ensuring a safe and secure travel experience is essential when visiting any destination, including Oslo. Here are some important safety tips to keep in mind:

Emergency Numbers:

One of the most important aspects of ensuring your safety while in Oslo is familiarizing yourself with the emergency contact numbers. The general emergency number in Norway is 112, which connects you to the police, fire department, and medical services. In case of a medical emergency, dialing 113 will directly connect you to the appropriate medical services. It is essential to have these numbers readily available, whether stored in your phone or written down in a easily accessible place. Additionally, it is advisable to have the contact details of your embassy or consulate in Oslo. This information can be helpful if you encounter any major difficulties or require assistance from your home country's diplomatic services.

Pickpocketing and Valuables:

While Oslo is generally considered a safe city, it is always wise to remain vigilant, especially in crowded areas and when using public transportation. Like in any popular tourist destination, pickpocketing can occur, particularly in busy tourist spots. To minimize the risk of falling victim to pickpockets, it is important to take certain precautions. Keep your belongings secure and within sight at all times. Opt for a sturdy bag that can be closed or fastened properly, preferably one that has additional security features such as anti-theft zippers or hidden compartments. Avoid carrying large sums of cash and only take the necessary amount for your immediate needs. It is also advisable to avoid displaying expensive jewelry or valuables that may attract unwanted attention. Consider using hotel safes or secure lockers to store valuable items when not needed. By being cautious and proactive, you can significantly reduce the risk of becoming a target for pickpockets.

Natural Hazards:

While Oslo is not prone to major natural disasters, it is still important to be aware of potential risks and take necessary precautions. The winter months in Oslo can bring snowy and icy conditions, leading to slippery surfaces. When walking on sidewalks or exploring outdoor areas, it is essential to exercise caution and wear appropriate footwear with good traction. Take your time and walk slowly to avoid slipping or falling. Pay attention to weather forecasts, particularly if you plan to engage in outdoor activities or travel outside the city. In case of severe weather conditions or safety advisories issued by local authorities, it is crucial to follow their instructions and take appropriate measures to ensure your safety. By staying informed and being prepared, you can navigate any potential natural hazards with confidence.

Respect Local Laws:

When visiting Oslo, it is vital to familiarize yourself with the local laws and regulations of Norway. Being aware of and abiding by these laws not only ensures your safety but also shows respect for the local culture and community. Here are some important legal considerations:

Smoking: Norway has strict regulations regarding smoking. Smoking is banned in all public indoor spaces, including restaurants, bars, shopping centers, and public transportation. It is important to adhere to these regulations and only smoke in designated outdoor areas or private residences where smoking is permitted.

Alcohol Consumption: It is illegal to drink alcohol in certain public areas in Norway, such as parks, streets, and public transportation. Drinking is generally restricted to licensed establishments such as bars, restaurants, and private residences. It is important to familiarize yourself with these regulations and consume alcohol responsibly within the designated areas.

Drug Laws: Norway has strict laws regarding drug possession and use. The use, possession, and trafficking of illegal drugs are strictly prohibited and can result in severe penalties, including imprisonment. It is essential to respect these laws and refrain from engaging in any illegal drug-related activities during your stay in Oslo.

Environmental Protection: Norway places a strong emphasis on environmental conservation, and it is important for visitors to respect and contribute to these efforts. Follow designated trails and paths when hiking or exploring nature reserves. Dispose of waste properly in designated bins, and avoid leaving any trace of your visit behind. Respect wildlife and their habitats by keeping a safe distance and refraining from feeding or disturbing them. Observe any guidelines or regulations set forth by local authorities in protected areas.

By familiarizing yourself with the local laws and regulations, you can ensure a smooth and enjoyable experience in Oslo while also demonstrating cultural sensitivity and environmental responsibility. It is always a good idea to research and educate yourself about the specific laws and regulations of the destination you are visiting to avoid any unintentional violations.

11.2. Money and Currency Exchange:

Understanding the currency and money matters in Oslo will ensure a smooth financial experience during your trip. Here's what you need to know:

Currency:

The currency used in Oslo, as well as throughout Norway, is the Norwegian Krone (NOK). Understanding the currency and how to handle it will ensure a smooth financial experience during your visit. Here are some key points to know about the currency:

Denominations: Norwegian coins are available in denominations of 1, 5, 10, and 20 kroner. These coins feature various designs and are easily recognizable by their size and appearance. Banknotes come in denominations of 50, 100, 200, 500, and 1000 kroner. Each denomination has a distinct color and features prominent Norwegian figures and landmarks.

Currency Symbols: The Norwegian Krone is represented by the symbol "kr" or "NOK." For example, 50 kroner would be written as "50 NOK" or "50 kr." When making cash payments or reading price tags, it's important to pay attention to the currency symbol to avoid any confusion.

Credit Cards and ATMs:

Credit and debit cards are widely accepted in Oslo, making it convenient for travelers to make payments without the need for large amounts of cash. Here are some important points to consider regarding credit cards and ATMs:

Acceptance: Visa and Mastercard are commonly accepted in most establishments, including restaurants, hotels, shops, and attractions. American Express and Diners Club are also accepted but may have slightly lower acceptance rates. It's always a good idea to carry a backup card from a different provider in case of any issues.

Informing Your Bank: Before traveling to Oslo, it is recommended to inform your bank or credit card company about your travel plans. This will help avoid any potential issues with your cards being blocked or flagged for suspicious activity. Informing them of your destination and travel dates ensures that your cards will work smoothly during your trip.

ATMs: ATMs, known as "Minibanks" in Norway, are easily accessible throughout Oslo. They can be found at banks, shopping centers, airports, and other convenient locations.

ATMs in Oslo typically offer an English language option for ease of use. It's important to check with your bank about any international withdrawal fees or daily withdrawal limits that may apply.

Currency Exchange:

Currency exchange services are available in Oslo at banks, exchange offices, and some hotels. Here are a few points to consider when exchanging currency:

Banks: Banks in Oslo generally offer competitive exchange rates. They may have specific hours of operation, so it's a good idea to check their opening times beforehand. Some banks may also require you to have an account with them to exchange currency.

Exchange Offices: Exchange offices, also known as "Currency Exchange" or "Forex" offices, can be found in popular tourist areas or near major transportation hubs in Oslo. These offices often have longer operating hours, making them convenient for exchanging currency outside of traditional banking hours. However, it's important to compare exchange rates and fees before making any conversions, as rates can vary between different establishments.

Hotels: Some hotels in Oslo may offer currency exchange services for their guests. However, it's important to note that hotel exchange rates may not always be as favorable as those at banks or dedicated exchange offices. If you choose to exchange currency at your hotel, it's advisable to inquire about the rates and any applicable fees beforehand.

Tipping:

In Norway, tipping is not mandatory, as service charges are generally included in the bill. However, if you receive exceptional service and wish to show your appreciation, leaving a small tip is customary. Here are a few guidelines to keep in mind regarding tipping in Oslo:

Rounding up the Bill: It's common practice to round up the bill to the nearest whole krone or add a small amount as a tip. For example, if your bill is 245 NOK, you can round it up to 250 NOK.

Percentage Tipping: If you prefer to tip a percentage of the total bill, a tip of 5-10% is generally considered appropriate for exceptional service. This is more common in upscale restaurants or for larger bills.

Service Charges: It's important to check your bill for any service charges or gratuities that may have already been included. Some establishments automatically add a service charge to the bill, especially for larger groups or in tourist-heavy areas. In such cases, additional tipping may not be necessary.

Tipping in Cash: It's worth noting that tipping in cash is appreciated, as it allows the server to receive the tip directly. However, tipping by card is also accepted and common in Oslo.

Remember that tipping in Norway is a gesture of appreciation rather than an obligation. The Norwegian service industry is known for its high standards, and tipping is not expected in the same way it may be in other countries.

Ultimately, it's up to your discretion whether to tip and how much, based on the quality of service you receive.

By familiarizing yourself with the currency, credit card usage, currency exchange options, and tipping customs, you can confidently manage your finances and transactions during your time in Oslo.

11.3. Local Customs and Etiquette:

Respecting local customs and practicing proper etiquette is essential when visiting Oslo to ensure positive interactions and a meaningful cultural experience. Here are some customs and etiquette guidelines to keep in mind:

Punctuality:

Norwegians place a high value on punctuality and appreciate others who do the same. Whether it's attending a meeting, joining a guided tour, or meeting up with friends, it's important to arrive on time. Being punctual shows respect for others' time and demonstrates your commitment to the engagement. If you anticipate being late, it is considered polite to inform the concerned parties in advance and provide an explanation for the delay.

Personal Space:

Norwegians generally appreciate their personal space and value privacy. When engaging in conversations, it's customary to maintain a comfortable distance from others. Avoid standing too close or invading someone's personal space unless explicitly invited or necessary. Physical contact, such as hugging or touching, is not common during initial greetings or casual encounters. Instead, a friendly handshake is the standard form of greeting in Norway.

Silence and Privacy:

Silence is often valued in public spaces in Norway, including public transport. It's customary to keep conversations at a moderate volume and avoid loud or disruptive behavior, especially when in enclosed spaces or quieter settings. Respecting others' need for privacy and quiet reflection contributes to a peaceful and harmonious atmosphere. Be mindful of the noise level when using public transportation or visiting places like museums, libraries, or churches.

Environmental Consciousness:

Norwegians have a strong commitment to environmental sustainability and place great importance on preserving their natural surroundings. It's essential to respect and support these values during your time in Oslo. Here are a few ways to contribute to environmental consciousness:

Recycling: Oslo has a well-established recycling system, with separate bins for paper, plastic, glass, and organic waste. Familiarize yourself with the recycling guidelines and dispose of your waste in the appropriate bins. Many accommodations and public spaces provide clear instructions for recycling, making it easy for visitors to participate.

Energy Conservation: Conserve energy by turning off lights, electronics, and heating when not in use. Practice water conservation by using water responsibly, especially in times of drought. Many hotels and accommodations in Oslo promote energy-efficient practices, such as using key cards to control electricity in rooms, encouraging guests to be mindful of their energy consumption.

Outdoor Ethics: When exploring Oslo's beautiful natural areas, such as parks, forests, or hiking trails, adhere to the principle of "Leave No Trace." Respect the environment by not littering and by carrying out any trash you generate. Stay on designated paths to minimize damage to vegetation and wildlife habitats. Avoid picking flowers or disturbing wildlife. Taking care of the natural environment ensures its preservation for future generations to enjoy.

By respecting local customs, practicing proper etiquette, and embracing environmentally conscious behaviors, you can contribute to a positive and harmonious experience in Oslo. These cultural nuances not only enhance your interactions with locals but also show your appreciation for the city and its values. Remember, embracing local customs is an opportunity to learn, grow, and foster cross-cultural understanding.

11.4. Language and Useful Phrases:

While English is widely spoken in Oslo, making an effort to learn and use basic Norwegian phrases can enhance your interactions and demonstrate respect for the local language and culture. Here are some useful expressions to familiarize yourself with:

Hello: "Hei" (pronounced hey)

This is a standard greeting used in both formal and informal settings. It's a simple and friendly way to initiate conversations.

Thank you: "Takk" (pronounced tahk)

Expressing gratitude is important in any culture. Use "takk" to show appreciation for a kind gesture, assistance, or service received.

Excuse me: "Unnskyld" (pronounced oon-skuld)

Use this phrase when you need to get someone's attention, apologize, or politely ask for assistance. It is a versatile expression that can be used in various situations.

Do you speak English?: "Snakker du engelsk?" (pronounced snah-ker doo eng-elsk)

If you find yourself in a situation where you need to communicate in English, this question can help you determine if the person you are speaking to understands English.

Please: "Vær så snill" (pronounced vair soh sneel)

"Vær så snill" is used to add politeness and consideration to a request or when asking for something. It's a courteous way to make your intentions clear.

Goodbye: "Ha det bra" (pronounced hah deh brah)

This is a common way to bid farewell. It can be used in both formal and informal settings, and it conveys the sentiment of wishing the person well.

Remember, Norwegians are generally welcoming and understanding, and many of them speak English fluently. However, making an effort to learn a few basic Norwegian phrases shows respect for the local language and culture. It can also help break the ice and create a more meaningful connection with locals.

If you're unsure about pronunciation or need help with the correct intonation, don't hesitate to ask for assistance. Norwegians are accustomed to foreigners learning their language and are usually patient and supportive. Embrace the opportunity to learn and practice Norwegian phrases during your time in Oslo, and you'll likely receive a warm response from the locals.

11.5. Oslo Travel Resources:

When exploring Oslo, having access to reliable travel resources and information can greatly enhance your experience. Here are some recommended resources to help you navigate the city and make the most of your visit:

Official Tourism Websites: Visit Oslo (www.visitoslo.com) and Visit Norway (www.visitnorway.com) are the official tourism websites that provide comprehensive information on attractions, events, accommodations, transportation, and practical tips for visiting Oslo. These websites offer detailed guides, maps, itineraries, and up-to-date information on current events and festivals happening in the city.

Travel Guides and Books: Travel guides specifically focused on Oslo or Norway can provide you with in-depth knowledge about the city's history, culture, attractions, and practical advice. Popular guidebook series like Lonely Planet,

Rough Guides, and Rick Steves offer detailed information, suggested itineraries, and insider tips to help you plan your visit to Oslo. These guidebooks are available in print and digital formats, making it convenient to carry them with you during your travels.

Online Forums and Travel Communities: Joining online travel forums and communities allows you to connect with fellow travelers, ask questions, and seek advice from those who have visited Oslo before. Platforms like TripAdvisor (www.tripadvisor.com) and Reddit's r/travel subreddit (www.reddit.com/r/travel) have dedicated sections where you can find discussions, recommendations, and firsthand experiences shared by travelers. These platforms can be valuable resources for getting insights into popular attractions, hidden gems, dining recommendations, and practical travel tips.

Mobile Apps: Install helpful travel apps on your smartphone to have instant access to useful information while exploring Oslo. Google Maps is a reliable navigation app that can help you find your way around the city and locate attractions, restaurants, and public transportation options. The VisitOSLO app, developed by the official tourism board, provides information about local attractions, events, restaurants, and offers interactive maps to help you navigate the city. Additionally, currency converter apps can help you stay updated on exchange rates and facilitate currency conversions during your trip.

Local Tourist Information Centers: Visit the local tourist information centers in Oslo to gather maps, brochures, and personalized assistance. The main tourist information center is located at Oslo Visitor Centre in Østbanehallen, adjacent to Oslo Central Station. Here, friendly staff members can provide you with information about the city's highlights, suggest itineraries based on your interests, and answer any questions you may have. They can also assist you in booking tours, acquiring transportation passes, or finding suitable accommodations.

By utilizing these travel resources, you can gather comprehensive information, plan your itinerary, discover hidden gems, and ensure a smooth and enjoyable visit to Oslo. Stay informed, take advantage of the wealth of information available, and make the most of your time in this vibrant and captivating city.

CHAPTER TWELVE

Conclusion

12.1Fond Farewell to Oslo

As your time in Oslo draws to a close, it's natural to feel a mix of nostalgia and gratitude for the memories you've created during your stay. Take a moment to reflect on the remarkable experiences you've had, the breathtaking sights you've seen, and the incredible people you've met along the way. Oslo's charm and beauty have woven their way into your heart, ensuring that a part of this Scandinavian gem will always remain with you.

Before you depart, take a leisurely stroll through the vibrant streets of Oslo's city center. Allow yourself to soak in the bustling energy, the harmonious blend of modern architecture and historic landmarks, and the lively atmosphere that permeates the air. Relish the opportunity to revisit some of your favorite attractions, letting their familiar presence evoke a sense of fondness and appreciation.

As you amble through the streets, consider making a stop at a local café for one last taste of Norway's renowned coffee culture. Order a steaming cup of rich Norwegian coffee and savor each sip, letting its comforting warmth fuel both your body and soul. Allow yourself to be fully present in the moment, taking in the sounds of laughter, the aroma of freshly brewed coffee, and the vibrant conversations that surround you.

Another way to bid farewell to Oslo is by immersing yourself in the serenity of its parks. Seek refuge amidst the lush greenery, finding solace in the tranquility they offer. Whether it's the sprawling grounds of Vigeland Park, where art and nature intertwine, or the peaceful oasis of Ekeberg Park, each step you take among the trees and flowers allows you to appreciate Oslo's commitment to preserving its natural beauty.

As you prepare to depart, take a moment to express your gratitude to the warm-hearted locals who have made your time in Oslo so memorable. The Norwegians' genuine hospitality, friendliness, and willingness to share their culture create an atmosphere of inclusiveness and warmth. Whether it was a helpful stranger offering directions, a passionate local guide sharing stories of their city, or a friendly conversation in a café, these interactions have left a lasting impression, making you feel welcome and appreciated throughout your entire stay.

Before you leave Oslo, consider seeking out mementos to commemorate your time in this remarkable city. Explore the charming boutique stores and bustling markets that dot the streets, offering a treasure trove of unique Norwegian handicrafts, intricate woodwork, and stylish Scandinavian designs. Whether it's a handcrafted piece of jewelry, a beautifully woven textile, or a piece of art that speaks to your soul, these souvenirs will serve as tangible reminders of the journey you undertook and the special moments you experienced in Oslo.

As you bid farewell to Oslo, take a moment to acknowledge the transformative effect this city has had on you. It has opened your eyes to new perspectives, broadened your understanding of Scandinavian culture, and enriched your sense of adventure. Oslo's allure will stay with you, resonating in your memories and beckoning you to return one day. As you journey onward, carry Oslo's spirit of discovery, warmth, and beauty within you, allowing it to shape future adventures and inspire a lifelong appreciation for this captivating city.

12.2. Oslo: A City to Remember

As you delve deeper into your reflections on your time in Oslo, the city's indelible mark becomes even more apparent. Oslo's allure lies in its ability to seamlessly weave together a rich history, breathtaking natural beauty, and a contemporary charm that captures the essence of modern Scandinavian life. These elements blend harmoniously, leaving a lasting impression that resonates long after you've bid farewell to its shores.

The iconic landmarks of Oslo stand as testaments to the city's captivating cultural and artistic heritage. The Royal Palace, with its majestic presence, offers a glimpse into Norway's royal lineage and serves as a reminder of the nation's rich history. Walking through the palace grounds evokes a sense of awe and wonder, allowing you to imagine the events that have unfolded within its walls.

Venturing further, you encounter the enchanting Vigeland Park, a haven of sculptures crafted by the talented Gustav Vigeland. The park's intricate statues depict the human experience, exploring themes of love, life, and human connections. Strolling through this outdoor gallery, you're filled with a profound sense of wonder, admiring the artistry and depth of emotion captured in each sculpture.

Oslo's vibrant museum scene adds another layer to the city's cultural tapestry. The Munch Museum, dedicated to the works of the renowned painter Edvard Munch, immerses you in his evocative masterpieces, from "The Scream" to "The Dance of Life." The museum provides a window into Munch's tormented soul and his unparalleled ability to convey raw human emotions through art.

For lovers of contemporary art, the Astrup Fearnley Museum of Modern Art beckons with its innovative exhibitions and thought-provoking installations. Here, you encounter cutting-edge works by both Norwegian and international artists, challenging your perspectives and expanding your understanding of artistic expression.

Oslo's outdoor adventures are equally unforgettable, offering a vast playground for exploration and relaxation. Sailing along the Oslo Fjord unveils breathtaking vistas of rugged coastlines, idyllic islands, and picturesque waterfront villages. The fjord's tranquil waters provide a serene backdrop as you immerse yourself in the beauty of nature.

The city's surrounding forests invite you to embark on invigorating hikes, where dappled sunlight filters through the trees, and the fragrance of pine fills the air. Trails lead you to hidden lakes, cascading waterfalls, and panoramic viewpoints that reward your efforts with awe-inspiring vistas.

During the winter months, Oslo transforms into a wonderland of snowy landscapes, offering a plethora of thrilling winter sports activities. Embrace the exhilaration of skiing down pristine slopes, navigate cross-country trails through enchanting forests, or try your hand at ice skating on frozen lakes. Oslo's winter adventures embrace the joys of the season, creating memories that will warm your heart for years to come.

No exploration of Oslo is complete without indulging in its tantalizing culinary scene. Norwegian cuisine delights your taste buds with a harmonious blend of traditional flavors and innovative culinary creations. Sample freshly caught seafood delicacies, from succulent salmon to delicate shrimp, expertly prepared to highlight their natural flavors. Savor hearty Scandinavian dishes, such as reindeer stew or fish soup, which offer a comforting taste of local traditions. Oslo's charming cafés and trendy restaurants provide the perfect setting to delight in the art of "fika" – enjoying a leisurely moment with a cup of coffee and a delicious pastry while immersing yourself in the cozy atmosphere of Nordic hospitality.

As you reflect on your time in Oslo, it becomes clear that this city has left an indelible mark on your soul. Its seamless fusion of history, natural beauty, artistic treasures, and culinary delights has created an experience that goes beyond mere travel. Oslo has awakened your senses, broadened your horizons, and instilled in you a profound appreciation for the city's unique blend of past and present. It is a place that lingers in your memory, beckoning you to return and continue exploring the depths of its captivating charm.

As day turns to night, Oslo transforms into a hub of vibrant nightlife and entertainment. Dive into the local bar scene, immerse yourself in live music performances, or dance the night away at energetic nightclubs. Oslo's nightlife ensures that your evenings are filled with excitement and camaraderie.

But beyond its attractions and activities, Oslo's true essence lies in the warmth and kindness of its people. The genuine hospitality and friendly nature of the locals make Oslo a city where you feel welcome and embraced. Their love for their city shines through as they share their stories, traditions, and unique way of life with you.

Oslo is a city that leaves an indelible mark on your soul. Its beauty, culture, and vibrant atmosphere create an experience that transcends mere travel. It becomes a part of who you are—a cherished memory that evokes a smile and a longing to return. Oslo is a city to remember, and it will forever hold a special place in your heart.

Printed in Great Britain
by Amazon